Zero Crunch

LEGAL NOTICES

Zero Crunch

The Best Way to Ethical, Cost Effective Software Development.

Mark Lloyd

Learning Points and Actions!

I don't know what it's like in your studio, but in my experience there is a better way to develop software, better for the team, better for creativity and for the bank balance! As you go through the book there are very specific learning points that will enable you to go to "battle with crunch". It doesn't need to win; it doesn't need to be the only way.

In Part 1 you will:

- Understand why development is hard, and begin to master it.

- Look crunch right in the face, know it, and plan to defeat it.

- Reveal the important difference between crunch and what overcoming development adversity is.

- Expose real costs of crunching and the damage it does.

In Part 2 you will:

- Explore the 3-Stage System, built through the hardest crunch and knowing what real teams are.

- Break each stage down and learn specific tools for specific problems.

- Manage change in the studio like never before.

- Finally, be able to work in a crunch free environment where success is not only fun but much easier.

Success is no longer about survival and damaging crunch, it's about you taking back control, and a new way of development.

Take the quiz to see if your studio and team are ready for a Zero Crunch way of working. Over at:

www.mlc-devsupport.com

TABLE OF CONTENTS

PART ONE:
Why is software development just so damn hard?

PART TWO:
Let's defeat crunch right now!

INTRODUCTION

Have you considered the possibility...?

T hat crunch is the single biggest threat to the long term future of development in any software environment?

In my experience it is. I have no doubt that it reduces creativity, drives burn out, it affects everyone, and it destroys teams. The worst part? For many studios and corporates, it's the only way they want or know how to build software.

It's time for you to take back control, develop software ethically and sustainably for you, the teams you work within and to safeguard the industry that we are part of, for generations to come.

Speaking of generations, I've worked so much crunch that at times I didn't understand the effect it had on my family, it felt like even Jodie, my dog, would forget who I was because I'd been working so much!

Dianne, my partner of 25 years, has endured all of the crunches I have, I know that now. When I was in the middle of it, I'm not sure I did.

The extended days both with early starts and late finishes meant that the only time we'd get together was when I'd quietly slide into bed late in the evening, exhausted. Or disturb Dianne getting up very early to be out and away to work. For months on end.

Stealing a day here or there and filling it with time-controlled activity, two hours with the family, an hour shopping, two hours watching a movie, only a little time to read the kids a bedtime story. All scripted, managed, trying to fit everything in because of someone else, some company's requirements.

I'd stopped being the person anyone comes to… you just aren't there for anyone, anymore…

I used to tell myself that it's "for the future," it's my job, my vocation, it's our future, both Dianne and I. Looking back, I had a vision and ambition, having that is so important. It's essential for all of us, right? An excellent stable occupation, something we can depend on?

I'd take all the great learning (the good bits, not the autocracy) from the forces and build real teams, bring some true efficiency and effectiveness to this industry that's still in its youth.

Be part of, and drive a team that everyone would know, the best they could be, working on the world's greatest video games. It wasn't just an occupation; it was a calling! I remember coming home once and saying to Dianne.

"Today was a great day, step 421 complete, toward global domination!"

Isn't it what we are all heading towards, what we desire?

However, what about those satisfying parts of your life that you have embedded as your comfort routines; that weekly walk in the park, going to the gym, visiting your favourite restaurant with your loved ones, date night, film night with the children, walking the dog?

All those everyday recreational activities that you have honed over months and years, the ones that make you feel safe, secure, happy. These times are the ones that you are working hard to fund, isn't that what working is about?

Generating enough money to live the way you want to, outside of work? If you are getting paid for something you love, for me, that is video games (later you'll read why), and you have quality time with your family then it's a perfect place to be.

An excellent job working on something meaningful that has a positive effect on the world, fun, educational. Earning the cash to support and nurture your family, being paid your worth and rewarded with recognition and responsibility, working with a purpose. What can be better? Financial stability allows a focus on the other areas of life, and to be happy.

Sounds amazing, but … Crunch takes over your life. Removes family time. Can you plan? Probably a day here or there, maybe you won't need to work extra that day, until 10 minutes before you leave work and you're asked.

Worse still, no day in the year is off limits to crunch; Bank Holidays, Easter, even Christmas?

It makes you start to hate your job, removes any capability to plan activity, family time should be spontaneous, shouldn't it? And crunch is often unpaid or certainly poorly rewarded.

Crunch will take you away from your children when they need you most, away from all of your family, even damage your marriage, or your most important relationships.

Working, earning, but with little or no work-life balance, what's the point? Crunch is the enemy; I know because it became "my" enemy.

Have no doubt that reading this book will mean you understand what real crunch is, and why it doesn't work for people, in the end, irrespective of how well a project does when released.

Prevent the damage before it evens starts, be part of the change the industry needs.

Now we already understand a little more, let's read on and go on the journey to Zero Crunch together!

PART ONE:

Why is software development just so damn hard?

CHAPTER 1

Making software is complex, understand that, and we are already winning.

Let's just get through today ...

You're sat at your desk, you've made a list of what you need to do, you hear the "ding" that signals another email is dropping into your inbox, helping the "unread" number to tick up mercilessly.

This last arriving email is going to be a call to a meeting, or a request for information, worst still some indication that there's a change to your work.

You daren't look, just ignore the email, and that little knot in your stomach ... when you heard it drop in.

I'm going to burn down my task list, that's where my comfort zone is ...

Bloody hell I need another coffee (rubs eyes), the commute was dreadful this morning.

Getting up in the dark in winter is always hard. Coming to work in the dark, going home in the dark ... depressing.

(Ding) ....

(Sigh), leave me alone! I'm sick of these 12-hour shifts. They promised us; they said four weeks.

I could manage four weeks of extended shifts, the game will be great, but we've been crunching now for three months.

I'd made plans for a holiday when the game was finished, a thank you to myself for what I had achieved as part of a good team on a great project. That seems a long way away now.

Will we ever be finished? I just can't see the end, more and more tasks added, even at this late stage ...

(reads the email) Meeting in 10 minutes ... changes to the schedule ... who can work more at the weekend ...?

No more. I'm going to look for something else, and I hope no one in I.T. is checking my search history. When this project is over, I'm off!

(gets a coffee, goes to the meeting, yes, it's yet another change meeting.)

Acceptance of the role you play and the development challenge.

As an engineer in my previous working life I understood the difficulty regarding physically tiring work, and in harsh conditions; when it's so cold outside, and you can't even feel your hands but have to put a spanner to good use.

Sitting in a warm office (well, unless you are under the air conditioning blower, we all know how that feels) seems more comfortable. It is, but development isn't about physicality, it's about keeping your brain engaged.

It is being able to think logically, creatively, consistently. To be able to understand what all the others around you are doing, how that affects your work, and how you change theirs. It's about focus.

Feeling like you are achieving for the project, the team, not being a burden, being recognised for a task well done.

All that is just challenging!

I'm not going to list the "White Papers" out there that prove diminishing productivity with additional hours worked. Adding creativity into the mix, logic, and problem solving, it's worse.

As a leader, you need to give space to those that are being creative, thinking, exploring, building. Those that fix, do tasks, they need time to grasp logic, to see the loops of development in the game. Build those core loops that mean the code is robust and lasts the test of time.

As a developer, if you have the time to be the best you can be, to defeat the biggest challenge for the studio, which is creativity hitting immovable deadlines, you need to be as accurate as you can with forecasting.

Be clear about where your knowledge is most reliable and the weakest. Be open about learning or where expertise is required so that it can be provided.

Team, team, team.

You're all trying to build something new, something unique, add that "secret sauce" that could make us all successful.

Be clear though; I'm not talking about the randomness of games like "Flappy Birds," you can't plan for that!

Two types of "unknown activity" to plan for, within the development process.

When we are trying to be creative, I think there's a desire to come up with something so different, so radical that creating that original element becomes a mountain to climb.

More often than not, and in an age of disruption (loosely, doing an acknowledged thing in a new way) the most successful software is based on something that has been incrementally improved. Windows, Apple iOS, are great examples.

The easier projects are those where a more significant amount of the code base, assets, design, have been created for previous versions. The choice for the next version is then generally about adding convenience, additional features for competitive advantage (to make people buy it) and a new look.

This way means that development is generally a balance of the "known unknown" (we'll use what we have but in a slightly different way) and "unknown unknown" (all the new functionality we will have to build from scratch).
I can't take credit for those descriptions, I've heard them a few times in the industry, but I believe they are good to use.

In video game terms we are talking about titles like Fifa, same fundamental game code base, new features, improved gameplay, new players and teams. A proven formula that means consistent release dates with better-understood development cycles.

You'd think they wouldn't have to crunch, well ....

The point is the more significant the "unknown unknown" component of your project, the more creation and change will occur as you are developing it.

Additional unknown elements need lots of planning up front! Let's accept that it's going to be challenging, that it's going to be time-consuming, that you will need to learn as you go.

The fact is, if you want to make something wholly new and innovative from a standing start, ground-breaking and genre-defining, it will take longer than you initially think to plan and execute.

A great example of what I think of as "late but amazing," is the original Max Payne. Arguably two years later than it should have been, groundbreaking in its realism and game mechanics.

Forty-two play throughs completed on Max Payne, working on the title directly, I still loved the "Bullet Time."

You'd think I'd be sick of it! Well ... no chance, I loved it!

Reducing the amount of "unknown unknown" will mean you have more chance of hitting deadlines and avoiding crunch.

So why do we make it hard for ourselves?

Later on, when we discuss managing change because when done poorly, is a significant driver of crunch, it will become clear how important understanding the volume of all unknown work is.

The critical mistake, leaders can make when saying yes.

Generally, when a studio is looking for work or has a great concept they want a publisher to pick up or an investor to finance, there is a tendency to go into high powered meetings with a tremendous amount of fear.

A bit like crunch, it becomes an "at any cost" scenario.

The promises flow! Saying yes to all the requests from around the table, "how about this?" and "it needs to be as successful as that."

Your whole focus is to put some cash in the bank so you can pay the team, keep the lights on and heat in the studio.

The trouble is, during that conversation, that you went in well prepared for (or so you thought) you hit a point where what you are nodding and agreeing to, is now outside the scope of your teams' knowledge and capability.

However, it's okay! We can recruit, we can move office, John (your industry mate) will help out.

None of which is true at that point, but how do you say no?

Well the problem is, and this is the mistake leaders make, you are now talking about planning, time, resource, cash, not just for creating the game but for all the additional setup items you've just made very simple - in your head.

Nine times out of ten you will:

- Underestimate the time it takes to hire the right people.
- Underestimate the amount of time and cost it takes to move and get set up.
- Overestimate John's availability as your go-to guy.
- Grossly underestimate the additional spend required to do all of the above.

- Massively underestimate the extra time, stress and pressure on you and the team to make this happen.

As you put your perspiring hand out to shake the cold, calm flesh of the most important person in the room, in effect giving a resounding yes, you feel like you've had a win!

Why then, as you walk back to the car, aren't you as happy as you should be?

In reality, you have signed up to their deadline for your delivery method, their milestones for their assumed development cycle and their release date based on other agendas and spending in which you have no say or part.

You did secure the money, right? All of the above is part of your "unknown unknown" project management process. Managing the lack of knowledge is the hardest part of the planning. If you have milestones to meet to get payments, did you actually secure that cash? Can you really deliver?

If you have experienced this situation, or if you fear this happening then read on, because the 3-Stage System will mean you can remove or reduce this effect.

If you manage to smash those meetings, in your favour every time, great! Still, read on because there is always useful incremental improvement.

Does all this sound familiar? If not, be warned.

The one thing I have learned after 20 years in software development, is that most development studios are built to be temporary.

Why? Because the real value is in the Intellectual Property that's created and the team that does the creating.

The rest? Rented office space with purchased technology: desks, chairs, and a fridge.

Inanimate objects have no value alone. Together they have the capability, but just like a car with the engine as its beating heart, development needs people at its centre.

So why, in an industry where the beating heart is its creative people, its creative capability, do we insist on smashing them on the rocks of crunch like a ship in a storm?

For those lucky ones reading this that haven't experienced crunch, but work in the software industry, take this as a warning that it has very little value in its most destructive form.

We are encouraged to grab any opportunity, but this can lead to overpromising and being woefully unable to deliver.

No good for reputation, repeat Work for Hire, or the team itself.

You'll read in many places in this book, that doing some overtime to get a project finished is pretty reasonable.

Creativity needs flexibility, and its why Agile project management works; tasks, sprints to catch up, managing the "unknown unknown" aspects, giving creativity the space it needs to be amazing.

Later I'll tell you a story of the tipping point I know we reached as a team working on GTA San Andreas. A personal tipping point that every developer, whole team, and leader has.

The story example at the very beginning of this chapter applies to any position in a studio, and whether you're managing or making assets for a project, emails become not only a distraction but a fear point.

For a coder, it could be an email from the Team Lead, for a Studio Head it could be an email from the Publisher.

During crunch, the fear is tenfold, because you are already working at your limit …

Learning Takeaway 1;

When developing software, we need to accept that there are many moving parts and change is inevitable. The most important thread running through this first chapter is people. It's people, including you, that choose the project, fund the project and build it.

If any of these people are without the correct knowledge, operating with fear, or believe it will be easy, then you are already starting from a negative position.

Questions – Make Notes:

1. *Think of an example project when you felt your planning wasn't strong enough to manage all those unknown changes, what happened?*
2. *Is there any fear within the team? Are you aware of it?*

CHAPTER 2

From fixing planes to video games, the learning! Who knew?

Finding my way to where I'm going ...
It's a warm and sunny morning, but then they all are when you're stood on an aircraft handling area at Muharraq Airbase in Bahrain, in the Middle East.

40 degrees C, it's 1991, and I'm standing with the other guys in the team in front of a large aircraft that's older than me. A Victor Mk2, a "V Bomber" from the late 40's, now turned into an inflight fuel tanker.

It's the first Gulf War and for right or wrong reasons as history now shows, the Royal Air Force was out in the Middle East doing what they do.

The politics and futility of war aside, being part of a team, doing tasks and engineering activity that could have fatal consequences if completed incorrectly was sobering. All this while having to carry weapons too, creates a pressure on a keen and driven 24-year-old, that's pretty heavy.

At that moment it didn't seem that way, we weren't in the direct firing line, unlike our Army brothers, out there in some sandy hole in the desert.

Or one of those front end units like the Chinook helicopter crews, that were inserting Special Forces into challenging places.

We in the main took it in our stride, and we'd had training, we had systems and structure, most of all we were a real team.

That feeling you get when the person next to you will be there come what may, it creates a bond. Now it doesn't mean that everyone gets on with everybody else all of the time.

Pressure creates conflict in people, the forces are no different, but we all understood there was a time to come together, and the laser focus on our objectives kicked in.

Little did I know at that point, that my desire to deliver would be a blessing when I entered the video games industry, but also somewhat of a curse. We'll come onto development "at any cost," I mean human cost, later.

Fast forward to 1999, and I'd done 13 years in the RAF as an aircraft engineer, most of my other friends that had left had stayed in the aviation industry. I chose to stay local to Lincoln, where my last tour in the RAF had ended. I had Dianne my partner and was settled.

Stood in mud, in a quarry in the fens of Lincolnshire, on my own, it's 4 am, it's cold and dark.

I'd been called out to work on a massive Volvo truck. This thing is busting my balls! Hours of trying to fix it!

I'd had enough I picked up my biggest spanner (£180 worth) and threw it as hard as I could into the depths and darkness of the quarry!

The sound of it swishing end over end, fading as it went into god knows where. Of course, it was the spanner I needed, the one I used a lot, and the only one of its type on my van. I'd thrown it a long way, and down into a big hole…

I was, done ….

I'd taken the role in a company called Pirtek two years earlier, a successful UK hydraulics franchise who had opened a depot in Lincoln.

'Mobile Sales and Service Technician' was my lofty title; basically, I had a van full of tools, and I'd drive around Lincolnshire fixing hydraulic equipment, from small through to the largest machines, dumper trucks with tyres taller than me!

When not fixing machines I was making sales — calling on suspicious Lincolnshire farmers that wouldn't even take a sample job for free!

"So Mr. farmer, pick one of your machines, and I'll change a hydraulic hose for free, so you can see how easy and quick it is."

"No, it's okay, I'm good thanks.'

"But that hose there on your tractor is worn, if that fails while you're using it, you could be injured, and there's downtime of course' (sell, sell)"

"No, no, it's all good, no need."

"It's err free, honestly, no commitment, if I never see you again, you got a hose for free."

"I'm good thanks, busy and all that, bye."

Basically, "don't let the farm gate hit your ass on the way out of my yard."

I wasn't too fond of this job, and it was depressing every time I got up in the morning. It was time for a change.

What had I learned from my fifteen years in engineering in both the military and civilian life?

- The systems in the military are tried and tested, efficient and effective.
- That real teams existed and could work under immense pressure and still achieve.
- That all projects and activities have an element of known and unknown activity.
- That systems in civilian life were different, more about minimum time, money and a smaller workforce.
- That there may not be a team, just you, or if there was a group, they could be only individuals together in one place.

- That planning, efficiency, and effectiveness were secondary to the business finances and winning more work than could possibly be delivered.

Learning Takeaway 2;

A real team has training, knows what it's capable of and why it's doing it. Every team member understands the particular part they play within the whole. Team members cannot be coerced. They need to want to be part of the team.

Questions – Make Notes:

1. *How do you build your teams? Is it a successful method?*
2. *Do they all know the part they play?*

The geek is strong in this one, Obi-Wan.

Why the games industry? Everyone asks. Well, my friends know that games have been my hobby and passion since I was a teenager.

From the day my Step-Father brought home a BBC Model B computer I was hooked!

To this day I don't know why, we were poor, he worked in a piston foundry, we lived on a council estate in Bradford. He just pitched up with it.

I was 15 years old, and the game it came with; Defender, the arcade classic, blew me away! Later on, we got Killer Gorilla (effectively Donkey Kong) and Chuckie Egg.

This experience was the start of my love of video games, it's all we talked about at school, and that was a good thing because a school in the 80's on a council estate in Bradford wasn't "all that" trust me!

Fast forward a little, two years to 1984, I'm 17, Bradford isn't brilliant, so I join the RAF to get away.

I'm going to make an assumption, most of you reading this book probably went on the same journey I did.

The one that spans many years of collecting machines, and playing video games. The fun, the excitement of new stuff.

Whether you're older like me or a student fresh out of University (you may even still be in Uni!) you've played many video games, or you're a bedroom coder, an artist that recreates those key characters from gaming history, or maybe you design multiplayer levels with your mates?

You'll understand this journey, and why I still play video games today. (Red Dead 2 and Assassin Creed Origins, at the time of writing this).

All through my time in the RAF my love of video games grew.

I bought various computers; Acorn Electron, ZX Spectrum, then the +2, the +3 (what a mistake that was).

Onwards into the next-gen, Atari ST, Amiga 600, all the while I stayed away from the console route mostly.

I didn't have a NES or a Megadrive, and I didn't know Mario or Sonic I was all about Speedball 2 and F1 GP.

Were you into computers or consoles? Alternatively, both?

I liked the complexity of the games on the computers, although little did I know that the consoles were generally where the polished and super fun titles were.

1998 and games were the only sane place I could go to while working at Pirtek. Remember? spanner thrown into the darkness, swish swish, hated every minute?

Doom, Heretic, and Settlers had been my go-to titles on my i386, now I was getting into Lucas Arts and X-wing vs. Tie-Fighter these games were unbelievably immersive.

I hadn't had as much fun since playing wireframe Elite on the Spectrum for hours, days, weeks.

Quake 1, Quake 2, Unreal Tournament, multiplayer clans, yes I was "that guy" who played on Christmas Day, even if it was just a clan training session.

You all know the feeling, the journey, the birth and growth of a new industry, a new time, video games were on the map!

Exit engineering... Enter the games industry. So it begins!

It's March 1999 I had quit Pirtek five weeks ago, I'd been looking for work.

The words of my former boss ringing in my ears and BIG lessons learned that would pay off later in my consultancy business.

I'm standing, in my oily overalls in the Pirtek depot, my Manager and the business owner in front of me.

(Read in a blunt, Doncaster accent)

"Ha! So, Mark, you're just going to quit without another job to go to?"

"Yes Terry, I'm done."

"Even though I promoted you to Branch Manager? I did that for you."

"No, you didn't want to lose me, so you did that for you."

"That's unfair."

"Maybe, maybe not, but what I do know is that we can't keep running this place the same way, you'll be out of business in a year."

"What would you know? I've run businesses for 30 years."

"Ok, thanks Terry, I'm going now."

"You won't get a good reference from me!"

"Ok, I understand."

He was true to his word about the reference, but luckily my next Manager at Tarantula Studios in Lincoln wouldn't take any notice of that particular phone call.

"Yes, very driven young man, but too headstrong, will never be a manager of people, doesn't understand them."

Ok, I'm so glad I managed not to fulfill that prediction!

Ahhh, it was so good knowing I wouldn't have to climb into the back of a big, half full dustbin lorry, stinking places those, and when I got out of the back where all the rubbish is, to have hair full of maggots! Retching the whole time I was doing that particular job.

Another valuable life lesson learned, those that don't want to change won't change, Pirtek in Lincoln changed owners three times in the next number of years. They made the mistake of underestimating the local competition that had been there 26 years, Pearson's Hydraulics. People by from people.

A lesson that I didn't always remember, many years on when talking to new prospects for my consultancy work.

I genuinely believe that when it comes to it, people know when they are doing something that in the end won't work. If that's the case, where is the motivation to do a great job?

The work becomes a transactional thing, some work for some money.

What I learned at Pirtek was that it doesn't matter how much someone says everything is okay and all right, that doesn't make it real.

When the people, the team, the leaders don't see a good outcome on the horizon that they can indeed be a part of and help work towards, how on earth are any of them going to be able to step up above and beyond to complete challenging work?

Fresh-faced and excited, as much as a 32-year-old can be as I completely changed my career from engineering. It was exciting! I had high expectations of it being very different.

Learning Takeaway 3;

If a team needs to work harder and do more than usual to achieve a goal, it needs to have a collective, agreed and communicated purpose — one that is both motivational, and intrinsically or extrinsically rewarding.

Questions – Make Notes:

1. *Are all your team members clear on the goal the studio is trying to achieve?*
2. *What do they say when they are asked to do additional work?*

The day the world fell in...

It's 2001, September, and by this time my small but
competent QA team had over two years under our belt at
Tarantula Studios, we numbered about fifteen then, and
we're working on multiple titles at once for not only
Tarantula but for Take 2 and Rockstar in general. We
were pretty independent of the developers' upstairs.

We had set ourselves up as a high-quality team even then,
and I had spent time with the Production crew and key
Senior Managers down in Windsor (European Head
Office) and made sure we had plenty to do, and they knew
who we were.

The systems we had built to test the projects were working
well. The key here was that we didn't have any industry
experienced people in our group, sure there was
experience upstairs in the dev team, but we were forging
our path, building our methodologies.

It's not a bad thing to bring in experienced people; it just
meant we had a clean standing start to build upon and
brought a new way to how we faced problems.

Maybe the next book will be about why you don't need a
200 strong QA team to test your titles (most out there),
just fewer, but outstanding people and equally good
systems and tools.

Then it happened ….

It was the afternoon in the UK, and one of the guys in
another room shouted;

"Come and look at this!"

We all ran into room 3 and stood around a small TV we used for testing and watched footage of an aircraft flying into the twin towers of the World Trade Centre.

Time seemed to stand still for a while, and I think anyone watching will have been shocked, we were. It's hard to know what to do at those times. As we continued watching, the towers collapsed one after the other, and it was disbelief really, how could buildings so big collapse like that?

It suddenly occurred to me that the Rockstar and Take 2 offices are on Broadway in New York, Lower Manhattan, near Soho, how were they being affected? Were they ok?

We had been working hard for a good few months on Grand Theft Auto 3, it was going to be groundbreaking, DMA Design (soon to be Rockstar North) were crunching, The New York team too, we were crunching hard, but this was the first 3D GTA, not the top down 2D fun fest of the previous two. This was big!

But, what now? What happens next?

My desk phone rang, I can't remember what time exactly, maybe 5 pm UK time, it was Sam Houser, the President of Rockstar Games.

Sam was instrumental in bringing GTA3 to the world, as were his brother Dan and other key figures in DMA Design (Rockstar North) in Edinburgh, Leslie Benzies, Arron Garbut, Andy Semple, and not forgetting the original DMA GTA team, David Jones, Mike Dailly, Russell Kay and Steve Hammond.

The conversation went pretty much like this.

"Mark!"

"Yes, Sam, what's happening over there? Everyone ok?"

"The world is falling in, dust clouds everywhere, they're shutting the offices!"

"Ok, what can we do to help?" (sounds futile in this situation)

"Look, GTA 3 has to come out on time, that means there are about four weeks left to get it finished." (yes, four weeks to submission with Sony as it's PS2, disc manufacture, then on the shelves by late October.)

"Yes, well we've been pushing hard on it, and so have the Edinburgh team."

"Mark, I don't know how long we will be closed here, or how much contact we'll have, so it will be the Edinburgh team and you guys that need to get this ready and finished."

"No problem Sam, we'll give it everything we've got!"

The New York QA team were "down," Edinburgh had a small QA team, and we were about fifteen heads, that's not many to finish up the testing on the first open world GTA in 3D.

However, we pushed hard, and we did it. The team were terrific, our systems and tools held up, we all felt immensely proud!

If ever there was a time to crunch, to step up for our displaced teammates in New York. To push on when there was so much sorrow in the city at that time, to help bring GTA 3 which was groundbreaking to the masses, to be a part of that history, it was now.

We did, the game launched on 22 October 2001, it was a massive success, it changed the industry, and the team and I did our bit.

That was our first big crunch, extended days, long weeks, months …

The learning? It needed to be "that crunch" at that time, I have no doubt, but the problem was it did become the way we at Rockstar made our industry defining games.

The problem is that it isn't sustainable, at least not for teams. It's really about knowing when the team needs to step up to get the project finished, but at the same time not smashing them into oblivion doing it.

It would be a while longer until I realized that, my dogged determination to succeed, to keep the studio and the team safe, in work, growing and prospering was the aim.

Our reputation (and mine) had grown; reliability, commitment, systems, security, and structure, were all active in the Lincoln team.

Everyone knew that now…

Learning Takeaway 4;

When the team rallies to overcome adversity, it galvanises them in a way that regular work doesn't. Individual and team capability is enhanced; the learning is locked in from the situation. Be warned; constant adversity is not sustainable for most individuals and teams.

Questions – Make Notes:

1. *When did the team in your studio come together behind a particular project to get it finished?*
2. *What improvements did you see come from that time?*

CHAPTER 3

When crunch actually became the bad guy in the room.

People are people, whatever the industry. For any software development studio knowing what crunch really means for your team is hard. I understand that, and I feel your pain!

Each will have a tolerance for additional work in the form of overtime in the evenings or at weekends.

Understanding this gets harder and harder as the team grows. How can a Senior Management Team possibly know all its people intimately enough to make sure that we don't overstretch them?

I'm not sure any Manager can be fully capable if they don't. But, that's my management style.

Maybe having to crunch to finish a project could be because the management team didn't know this one fact well enough?

I think this can stem from not appreciating how vital recruitment is from a team perspective. How do we make an already excellent team scale and be as effective?

In engineering terms, there's a bit of science to do with metals called "the elastic limit."

This measurement is the point of no return when you stretch a piece of metal just before it breaks.

If you remember as a kid, those Refresher chews, you could stretch them, and they would go thinner and whiter in the middle and stay pulled.

When you stretch metal, it will go back to pretty much its original size until you reach its elastic limit. When it stays stretched and doesn't go back to it's original state.

At this point the metal is weak, any amount of additional force is likely to end up in failure and breakage.

For aircraft this is catastrophic, but I believe the same applies to people.

Have you considered the possibility that people can be crunched to their limit, and from that point forward any crunch however small is capable of breaking them?

Growing your team is a meaningful and challenging process that's more about people than skills.

There's a concept that originated in the 1960s and was later developed by American academic Denise Rousseau.

"The psychological contract represents the mutual beliefs, perceptions, and informal obligations between an employer and an employee.

It sets the dynamics for the relationship and defines the detailed practicality of the work to be done."

Why is the psychological contract so much more important than a transactional (work for pay) one? Because in a creative environment, teams need to feel connected, happy and that everyone in the group gets treated fairly and equitably.

When this is in place amongst the team members and with their managers, the desire to give a little more when there's a need is real, to help, assist, to repay in kind.

This contract is earned and built in the same way respect is. It won't be forced. It's how real teams are formed.

Humour coupled with the generosity of time and knowledge, understanding, empathy, sharing without agenda. These are the kind of traits and interactions that build the psychological contract over and above the transactional.

This unseen, unwritten contract amongst the team and its leaders gives a resilience that makes a studio ready for growth; new people, systems, culture and all built on the rock-steady foundation of trust and commitment.

Without the psychological contract in place and healthy within a studio, I fear the team is only working at their minimum transactional capacity, and creativity is at its weakest.

What fast growth looked like?

Sat in a hotel bar in San Francisco, drinking Mount Gay rum and coke with a Producer friend.

Part of a US tour promoting release titles for Take 2 Interactive, that year. Reflecting on the last two years, the changes had been felt by the Lincoln crew. We numbered about 35 now, firmly settled inside the Take 2/Rockstar world as a critical QA and European Production team that supported the whole company.

The most significant change in those two years since GTA 3 happened earlier in the year, involved a meeting with the development team Leads back home, to find out that Tarantula Studios, our management studio, had been instructed to do a buyout within three months or they would be shut down by the publisher!

Not good news, I remember feeling sick to my stomach, all we had built, the team, the jobs. We weren't just supporting the studios here on site, but testing projects from all over the company, globally.

Then, sadness followed by relief.

"What about the QA team?"

"You QA guys are fine and aren't part of this."

Was the message from Steve, Tarantula's, Studio Head.

A few weeks had gone by since that meeting, and it was critical that we as the QA group continued to support all the studios we were working with, in the best way.

We had dodged a bullet ....

The buyout didn't happen. Via a phone call, I'd been told by my new manager to help the team upstairs move out. I was to move the QA team upstairs, as there was more space.

Damn! Not a good job, I hated it, we were friends with these guys I knew them all pretty well, but the industry is cutthroat like that.

This industry cycles studios and people almost continuously and at that moment in this new age of video games (in its youth really), there was a tendency for all the senior people in larger publishers to have sales rather than creative backgrounds.

Box sales were King, if they fell off, then you as a studio were probably, finished.

Missed deadlines and teams damaged by crunch, didn't help prevent this outcome, creativity and innovation are critical in the game industry, and crisis hurts both.

Life as a studio development team could be very short if you were labeled as underperforming.

We had moved in upstairs, expanded to the current 35 people. It was becoming clear to me that my "seat of the pants" management style, the learning from the military and the last four years weren't going to be quite enough to drive onwards and upwards.

I needed help, most of us do at some point, simply more learning required.

It had been a long time since I had done any academic study, the last being aeronautical studies twelve years before when I entered the RAF, but I had to, so I started my learning journey to get a Master's in Business.

If I was going to work for the team and negotiate with the most critical people in the company, I needed to know what they did about business, think as they did, talk like they did.

We all know what that's like, high powered meetings, feeling like you're stood in front of those characters holding all the cards, with your pants down!

Back at the bar in San Fran, five or six rum's down, a great friend of mine, Graeme Struthers, a true games industry veteran and then Head of Development for Europe, came and sat next to us.

"Lloydy…" *(a nickname carryover from my military days)*

"Kelly (Kelly Sumner, CEO of Take 2) has just been on the phone; he wants you to put a proposal together for growth in Lincoln, so your team can do QA for the whole of Take 2 and Rockstar."

"Oh! Err ok, Great! When?"

"Now…" *(Graeme lets out a little chuckle)*

"Damn! Really? I've had a few rums!"

"Doesn't matter mate."

"Ok, can I borrow your laptop?"

"Sure, here's my room key, mail the doc to me when you've done it, I'll send it straight to Kelly."

I rode the lift to my room on the 13th floor looking out over San Francisco downtown, opened the borrowed laptop, and started building a proposal for expanding the Lincoln Studio. Four hours and fifteen pages later with much coffee drunk, I emailed the completed document.

The next day Kelly Sumner …

Said, yes.

I'm sure this decision in part had been down to the Lincoln crew smashing the testing of Grand Theft Auto Vice City out of the park, last year. You're talking about a game that sold over 17.5 million copies worldwide by 2008 and netted north of half a billion dollars in sales. Our reputation was gold as the go-to QA team.

Team size doubled to 65, new building, new equipment, beefed up security. All the systems and structure from day one back in 1999. Incrementally improved, tested and proven under the harshest development conditions and now also the company experts in multi-lingual localisation testing.

Lincoln was well and truly on the global map for the company, and we had worked on dozens of titles, platform skus, language skus and more.

We even started doing the full production role on many of the lower level Take 2 titles in Europe, working directly with the 3rd party dev teams to get their products finished and out on time.

Five years of hard work in, and many of the first team members were still working in Lincoln. Four of the original six team members and something like twelve of the first fifteen recruited within six months of setup.

So the real team was deployed and working, the learning, the systems had all paid off.

Our turnover of less than 10% and lower sickness was unheard of in an industry QA group. All this with the reputation of the hardest and longest crunches.

Working hard was pretty much a badge of honour …

Today, with more than a decade of hindsight it's not the way to work, and even back then it was already feeling somewhat unsustainable, there had to be a better way to make video games?

Right?

Learning Takeaway 5;

Growth requirements may not always be obvious and get missed or may be called for when there is no real need. Panic creates both of those states. Growth should be a necessity, but the key is to know when by paying attention to output levels.

Real growth is built on a strong foundation of previous incremental improvement. It's rarely stable long term built in any other way.

Questions – Make Notes:

1. What was the last growth phase you or your studio went through? What were the drivers?
2. Discuss with the team members involved how successful they thought that growth phase was.

GTA San Andreas – when crunch began to really hurt...

San Andreas is arguably the best and most important GTA that has been released to date, a number of people believe that fact. (27.5 million copies sold worldwide, reported by Kotaku in 2011).

It was massive not only regarding success but in the scope and range of gameplay, the size of the game world, the humour, the music.

Everyone was playing it. For me, it was something that made me proud. The testing was a massive undertaking and in multiple languages as always.

This cycle represented the most prolonged and sustained crunch we had done so far.

We had teams in 24/7, split shifts, 12 hours minimum for everyone, the whole crunch lasted about four months. By comparison to later crunch periods, this was short.

Fifteen hour days were regular, so I could do the handovers at shift change day and night,

8 am and 8 pm (7 pm – 10 pm daily). However, worst of all, in the four months (120 days) of daily crunch, I had only two whole days off ...

I can't believe it myself when I say it, Dianne my long-suffering partner will always confirm that point back to me, other members of my team did the same or similar kinds of hours. If you've ever crunched, you know how that feels, explaining to the family that you're working again, and again and again.

The US time difference, the enormity of the project, the size of the bug database all contributed to the "always on" requirement to get the work done.

As a pretty stout fellow, circa 17 stone when I'm somewhat fit, in that four months of takeaways, little sleep, no home life, I put on three stone. I was fat, unhappy, tired and now 20 stone.

What a mess, my team were broken, smashed. The game released, it broke records, it became the game of a generation. We had indeed gone above and beyond.

However, at what cost?

From that point on, no one in the Lincoln team would work seven days a week; everyone would get a day off at least. Yes, six days, that's still too much, but we had to keep studio growth and momentum going. Jobs, livelihoods, mortgages depended on it.

There had to be a better way ... A feeling confirmed by this phase of development.

Just to be clear on a few things.

I am not an advocate of crunch, that's becoming clearer as you read this book. I think there is a better way to develop software. On the ground, "in the trenches" the damage caused by crunch to people, families and the lost time is very tangible.

The time I spent with Rockstar, the people in Lincoln, the effort, the work, it was and I hope is still, a real team.

We came together with little or no games industry experience, but we were gamers to the core, we built systems, structure, we expanded our capability and the team.

That team has been part of and worked on some of the world's greatest video games. They have defined a generation, GTA, Max Payne, Red Dead, well over a hundred million people have played them, laughed, maybe cried and been on a journey with those games.

I am immensely proud to have been part of that, and the global work the whole Rockstar Games team have achieved. I always will be. Now, many years on, with an expectation and experience that crunch is damaging, it's time to do it differently.

For every studio out there, whether large or small, or just starting, how you build your team, your systems and the culture you embrace, will drive whether you have to crunch, or be part of a new way of development …

Learning Takeaway 6;

It doesn't matter how good the team or individuals are, or how vital the work is; there is a saturation point for people and groups. When reached the work output starts to fall. The excess work damages the team and the desire and ability to go harder and do more next time is always diminished.

Questions – Make Notes:

1. *Identify when the team and studio last crunched to get a project finished, a project when the additional time seemed excessive.*
2. *What were the effects on the team, during the crunch and then afterwards?*

CHAPTER 4

Let's learn what crunch really is, so we can defeat it!

C runch is many things to many people, but we need to define it for clarity.
Crunch has become one of the most overused words in the games industry. In fact, it's used in all the varied software development environments, whether its games, web, apps, business or enterprise software.

It's talked about as part of University games development courses as an industry phenomenon. Abertay University in Dundee who have an excellent set of games courses and reputation feed the industry with strong graduates, and tell all their games students about crunch.

The trouble is, there isn't one specific definition as far as I know. However, there are hundreds possibly thousands of comments, articles and white papers that all see crunch as a harmful activity when it comes to development.

I'm going to define what crunch is, in one sentence.

'Crunch is that period towards the end of a project, when overtime and additional hours, weeks and days are the norm. Usually enforced, often unpaid to complete project tasks and get to a mutually all party agreed finish point for software.'

I'm a firm believer that a specific amount of overtime done on a project does not always constitute crunch. Overtime is a fundamental part of working life all around the globe in all industries and disciplines.

The fact is that when activity happens in a work environment, there is always an element of the unknown that makes it truly impossible to plan everything down to the smallest detail.

If we accept that fact, there is an additional and critical creative factor that reinforces overtime.

The most significant single reason crunch exists within the games development industry is that:

'When the need to be creative and build new and exciting software, comes up against agreed delivery deadlines that are hard to move and driven by heavy spending in other areas, then additional work is inevitable.'

That sentence adds weight to itself exponentially when you increase the size, scope, and creativity of any individual project.

In my experience the consensus about a crunch period in terms of the activity when it begins, is this:

- It's the time at the end of a project where creativity takes a back seat, and finishing is vital.
- Any time, resource and methods are deployed to get the project to that finish point.
- It takes a toll on the people, the work, the quality, the demotivation is palpable.
- It might even mean reverting to MVP (minimum viable product).
- It has no boundaries in terms of hours, days, weeks, months even years!
- It appears to be only driven by financial gain.

The worst feeling a leader has...

If you are a good manager, a leader, I'm going to assume you are, because if you're reading this book, you want to do things in a better way. You may have experienced this feeling.

If you aren't a leader but are in the industry and want to know what crunch is but don't like the concept, if you follow the 3-Stage System in this book, you will become a leader; I have no doubt.

What I'm going to tell you next is essential, because any person who is not a robot and has any empathy, will not want to be in this position.

The most soul-destroying thing that can happen is when one of your best team members, with vast knowledge, an outstanding performer and possibly even close friend who's worked with you for years, knocks on the door and comes in with that piece of paper in their hand.

You know, the one that looks like a resignation letter …

The fear hits you, your mind races, why? Why now? What have I done? Why didn't I see this coming? How am I going to replace them?

They sit down, and it feels emotional, it is emotional!

They start by saying;

"Sorry… But I'm handing in my notice."

There's that moment's silence, and you want to say no! However, you know that if this person, a critical team member, a friend, the "through thick and thin" type has got to this point, it's too late.

They've given you many chances, and you were asleep at the wheel, you didn't see it coming.

Maybe you were crunching too and were just so tired. Perhaps just too many crunch periods meant this was the final straw for them.

It's irrelevant now, you try and save the relationship, the situation, but all you end up talking about is the arrangements for a great send off, a leaving party to remember …

This particular team member got to their "elastic limit" went past it and is broken… You missed it.

If you've been there and you care, these are leadership failures that stay with you.

That's why I know what it does, and how it makes you feel …

What are the team effects? What situations will I find myself in?

For the team, the worst effect is that they have to watch good and talented people walk out of the door, their friends and comrades because they are burnt out and angry.

How will that strength in the team be replaced? That knowledge? That steady hand that was there when you needed it the most?

What about those that stayed? When the call comes in from the client, publishers, bosses requesting more crunch because of change, how are you as the leader going to ask the team?

Imagine standing in front of the whole team, and they're all looking to you.

"I've just had New York on the phone."

(I can't help but look down at the floor for a moment)

"The release date has moved, the game isn't ready, we already knew it was going that way."

(silence in the room)

"We are going to have to push on and work harder to get this done."

(the sighs, the looks, everyone is looking at the floor now)

You give your best speech, you know that the team will step up, they always do, and so do you. But how do you feel? How do they feel?

Awful.

Then it gets worse.

Crunch is not only creating disharmony in the team, but some start to drop to just the transactional working hours. All goodwill is beginning to wane.

The psychological contract you've spent years building is crumbling.

As team changeover becomes inevitable, fresh blood, how do we stop them being affected by a now disgruntled team? Apply more pressure? More authority? This will only create a downward spiral.

Not only that but how is any Project Manager/Producer supposed to know the actual capability of the team when it's in a state of constant change? All planning becomes a best guess.

A reputation for high turnover in an industry coupled with crunch is not good! Some companies create games "forged in the fire of crunch," I know I worked for one.

However, you then raise the question ....

Just how ethical is this?

When it gets to the point where that bit extra to catch up on a sprint or a deadline is over, and you enter real crunch you are damaging the work-life balance of the people with which you work.

You are affecting their families, possibly their income, and their well-being.

If that is as familiar to you as it is to me, then you know exactly why I wrote this book, why I've created a system to smash crunch in your development team and how to give studio leaders the knowledge and capability to say yes to the right projects for the team.

If this isn't familiar and you're new to the industry, then the 3-Stage System is like laying the most substantial foundation block for team happiness, stable growth, and success.

Learning Takeaway 7;

Adding or extending crunch within teams has little or no positive benefit beyond ticking off tasks in a project plan. Within teams it creates resentment, both of others and the work and also the managers that impose it.

To maintain an extended crunch requires a continuous and increasing de-motivational control that descends into micromanagement. Which only has any small amount of value at the point of team destruction. Do this and there is nothing left for the next project.

Questions – Make Notes:

1. *Have there been times within your studio where the additional time became forced and non negotiable? Discuss which projects that happened on.*
2. *What changes did you make from any learning that came out of that most challenging crunch?*

___

CHAPTER 5

Cost and costs; cold hard cash, quality and sanity too.

What makes a best seller? A creative piece of genius? A money spinner?
One of the key drivers in the games industry, in fact in any industry is the need and desire to make money.

There is a thought floating around out there in the minds of creative people that they "just want to create."

I always think it's like musical artists; they create their first album, it's content is heavily driven by the industry and its desires, the latest trends, the current sounds that are getting traction.

It needs to meet the marketing expectations, the label's agendas, the shareholders and their financial stake requirements. The messaging is "you can't do it without us." For a musical artist's first album, this is probably pretty accurate.

We are however all aware of those social media sensations that rise to fame via YouTube or similar. One gazillion views and climbing.

I still think they are rare.

It's more about the X-Factor method, a prospect, a chance, and a large team of experts with a PR and Publishing Machine behind them.

Then we get to the second album, you know, the one that they want to make that's really their music, their creative vision because they're a "big seller" now. This can be a push back on the formula of the label. It also happens when an artist is so established and famous that they can make pretty much what they want.

Not sure about you, but often it's miles away from why I liked them and the first album. Being creative and following your own vision is no guarantee of financial success.

The games industry and software development, in general, is no different.

Creativity is the aim, developing the best game in the world, the most successful, but this as with many things requires money to fund it. With money given (or borrowed), outside control of what a studio creates is never far away.

Many studios make the game that they want, and it gets little or no traction and runs at a loss.

Even in 2019 the biggest selling games out there are owned and developed by the world's biggest publishers. They have the money to create the next version of any particular title.

I remember back in the early 2000s when any game title that sold more than a million units was considered "AAA." This status pretty much guaranteed a sequel and would keep doing so as long as it retained that status from sales.

These days, I'm not sure that even exists, or at least in the same way in the boardrooms around the world, if the most significant games don't make 10 million sales, more, they are seen as failures for the corporation.

When half a billion dollars is a failure by the year end because it should have been a billion …

The pressure of the income expected from sales, the spend on marketing and PR, the expected salaries, the dividends on stocks. Money, money, money!

In reality, there may only be 6 degrees of separation from the board of a corporation down to a coder in a development studio i.e. where the money begins and ends.

The top level? Board Member; The Billion-dollar game requirement and pressure, for the largest publishers in the world, followed by …

CEO of the Publisher, to CFO of the Publisher, to Global Head of Dev, to Studio Head, to Code Lead, to Coder.

The message?

"You need to work as hard as you can because we need to meet the requirements and promises made to everyone on this list."

Unfortunately, for development teams in any software environment, the stakes are so high that a culture of 'at any cost' is fostered, or worse imposed; time, brain cells, creativity, family, all lost, the things we know that we give up when we crunch.

Crunch at its very worst, the pain we overcome and the extra time we give to make people various degrees of separation away from us, very wealthy. Our creative drive, our blood, sweat, and tears to pay dividends to a financial institution that owns stock in the publisher and doesn't even know (or care) who we are.

This is the kind of crunch that I remember at Rockstar.

Now, for a bit of balance, when a game did well, the teams that worked on it usually got some level of reward: more cash, a bonus, a better studio, better activities. Indeed, in my experience that's been the case.

Ok, it's all relative, especially financially but the West is generally seen as a meritocracy, my journey started on a Council Estate in Bradford from challenging home life and little education.

Work hard, do well, is the mantra. However, let's not forget the money, the cost, the reward and how that affects creativity, project delivery, and the teams.

I get it, so what's the problem on the cold hard cash front?

It's all fine and good when a game release is a success. What about when it's a failure? What I mean by failure is that it didn't do "as well as expected."

I'm not sure what that actually means, an actual measure as it's usually driven by expectation, best guess and a need to boost a share price!

However, it's often the answer given by a Publisher when the studio asks that question.

For most studios that are Publisher funded there's a complex equation that hits a tipping point when a studio can win financially, after the Publisher or financier has met their costs and obligations.

What if that tipping point isn't reached? That magic number?

How does this manifest itself for the development team on the ground who have crunched for months?

- Overtime is unpaid.
- Studio and team can be seen to have failed.
- Studio budgets may be affected.
- Future projects may be in doubt.
- No bonus paid.
- No financial benefit to team members or their families.

In the worst case scenario, members of a development team may experience everything in the list above, and then the studio could be closed or not receive further funding from its backers.

All this on the back of working as hard as you can in a crunch, to get a project finished.

It's soul and self-esteem destroying ...

Don't think I'm somehow condoning or avoiding what happens with failure; I'm not. Poor creativity and weak project management leading to crunch will always mean that what gets released is less than the vision of all parties, costs more, takes longer and is, therefore, less likely to succeed.

The balance comes with the right planning, project management, team makeup, appropriate time and budget coupled with reasonable expectation for the funders and publishers.

Sounds easy in one or two paragraphs, we all know it isn't, but if you aren't thinking about being better as a studio or publisher at all of these stages, it probably won't go as you expect.

Isn't it different for Indie studios?

Not really, generally, independent studios especially the smaller ones are operating on tighter budgets.

Whether it's Work for Hire or their own I.P., there will always be pressure to crunch to meet the next milestone or deadline, pass it and get payment. Alternatively, with Work for Hire a team can also feel or experience crunch by proxy, via the client and the pressure they feel to get a project finished.

Big titles and big publishers seem to think they need crunch to meet fixed release dates, marketing spends, shareholder expectations.
Interestingly I think managing crunch can be much harder for indies if they are looking to grow.

Much of the talent out there on the market, those that smaller indies can afford, are often from previously closed studios or have been smashed by a crunch.

This means any desire or requirement for a studio leader to ask a team member for overtime can be challenging. Especially if you can't get anyone to work harder and do more in a productive and team enhancing way, because they are already burnt out.

Many individual developers know what they are getting into when they join a larger or Publisher owned studio, crunch is inevitable. (in most cases)

Indies often learn all this the hard way.

___

Learning Takeaway 8;

While creativity is what makes the games industry special, money is what makes development possible. Having balance in terms of understanding a teams' capability and therefore its cash worth to a client is important.

The right amount of money to get the right team in place, assure quality and on time delivery, helps avoid crunch.

Questions – Make Notes:

1. *Has your studio found itself in a situation where the money became tight? What happened?*
2. *What projects in the studio have proven lucrative for the development team? What do you think made them financially successful?*

What about the quality cost?

Having worked in QA for over a decade, I've never understood the industry's stance on testing.

It, without a shadow of a doubt, is seen as either the "bit at the end" or a necessary evil.

I can hear some of you saying.

"No! I've never thought of it like that!"

Ok, I'll accept there are some of you that are QA Evangelists (like me), that understand the need and the power of good quality assurance.

Here are a few key reasons why a development team needs to take testing very seriously.

Without proper testing, your amazing game won't work and isn't yet finished.

Continuous test cycles, time and cost, pressure on the scheduling. Developers become frustrated.

Without adequate testing, when your game is released, many more people will be playing it and find the issues that you didn't. All those problems encountered by the users will mean additional cost, time, team and more, taking away from what you are currently doing because you thought you had finished.

Without quality assurance across the whole development phase, the assets, whatever the type aren't robust enough for extended or repeat use in future projects.

In the worst cases, all this can lead to brand damage, bad press, user frustration, as well as all the extra time and cost. Oh, and crunch of course.

Inadequate or missing testing of your project is one of the most significant contributors to crunch in the industry.

"You thought you were finished, well... there's all these fixes to make because of bugs the public found, patches to create."

'Right first time' is a hard place to get to in such a creative industry, but it does need to be the aim.

A little football analogy for you …

Your Coders. Artists, Designers are the Strikers and Midfield players in the football team. They score the goals, create the opportunities, feed the ball.

The Game Producers/Project Managers are the Defenders, supporting the team, keeping the win on track, bringing safety.

QA (the testers), they are the Goalkeeper, the last line. They are at fault when they let in a goal and usually get some blame.

However, if they aren't there, then it wouldn't matter how many goals are scored up front by the strikers, an open goal mouth at your team's end will mean you will probably lose the match.

There's one fundamental weakness in this analogy; we talk about QA in software development as if it's a team or single process. The testers carry out the QA; the testing often comes at the end.

That's a mistake, and a common one in development. Testing isn't glamorous, it's the opposite of creating, but we are talking about Quality Assurance.

We use the word assurance very easily, but if you think about what that word means then the responsibility for quality falls on everyone and everything you develop.

Quality is a thread that runs through the whole team, the entire process, each task, each milestone. Otherwise, there is no assurance of anything.

Going back to our football analogy, every member of that team to a man, whatever their role; going forward to score always gets back to defend, to support the Goalkeeper in the box, to try and prevent the other team scoring.

In development, part of any role; coder, artist, designer, sound engineer, is to try and make sure that they not only produce high-quality work but that it behaves as expected.

This means creating and testing as we go. We are assuring quality with each task completed, passing your best work assets on to the next person, building strength on strength.

Not only does this make you feel great, actually knowing that a piece of work is indeed complete, but that component of code or art asset may be used over and over. It becomes a cornerstone of what and how things are built in your future projects. It's reliable.

When the team doesn't embrace quality testing and assurance, then the symptoms are evident in the key reasons mentioned.

One other observation I've made and will compound the problems above.

When teams and developers are in a crunch, the first thing they will cut from their routines and tasks is testing what they have built. They are so focused on creating what any particular task requires, that when that's done they need to back themselves to say

"It's ok, it will work as needed, yes, it's the right quality."

The result? The test team finds problems with it, they report it, and we are into the "games not finished". They don't find the issues; small test teams, developers dropping testing, then we are into requiring post-release patches.

Weak assets have their own problems; when you come to use those assets, that code or that method of developing next time, it may have to be redone, rewritten, because it was weak in the first place.

Teams get tired; creativity is damaged; the whole situation compounds itself! It's a downward spiral of crunch.
The message?

Support the Goalkeeper; you are a team, your QA systems are for all, you are all working together to win that match.

If you are one of those teams that truly understands quality assurance within your development cycles, you have a "culture of quality", then you will be enjoying the benefits of one of the key pillars of activity that can reduce or defeat crunch.

Let's now look at another pillar; understanding and managing change when it hits your project.

Learning Takeaway 9;

Quality assurance is at the heart of not only being effective in your development, but has a positive effect on efficiency too. "Right first time" can be rare in software development, it's creative, it needs to evolve, but assets built with high quality will always serve a team and project better. Assuring quality needs to be embedded in the culture and systemized in the most efficient way, so that it's easy to embrace.

Questions – Make Notes:

1. *Can you think of a time when quality let the studio or a project down? Discuss with the team.*
2. *What did you do or put in place to make sure that didn't happen again?*

_____

CHAPTER 6

How can we get out in front, and ride that wave of efficiency?

Ahhh, that dreaded "change" word.
One of the biggest challenges, as we've discussed is managing change. Any change, from any situation.

Problem is a number of the changes that hit a studio often come from outside, and a team can only respond, try and make it happen.

However, when we think about it, when the change is instigated by the team and inside the team, then surely the response can be measured and managed?

It's changing... but on our terms.

Later in the book we will explore methods to manage change, not least of all understanding and exploring why there is a need to change before actually starting to make it.

For this chapter we'll keep our thinking light, there are hundreds of books out there that talk about change management. I'd like to simplify it at this point, take away its power to drive fear!

Imagine in your head an equilateral triangle. At each of the 3 corners there is a word. (this is a variation of the Project Management Triangle).

- **Time** (creation and tasks).
- **Resource** (people and cash).
- **Output** (quality and size/scope).

If the triangle balance is disrupted (all sides equal), i.e. one of those 3 areas changes, the other's must change accordingly and come back to balance to deliver the agreed project on time and budget without crunch and with the required quality.

Here's a story about how a few friends and I changed the way we did our planning because of the unknown aspects of a particular excursion we were taking a good few years ago, that threw our planning triangle off track from a time and output perspective.

It's 4:30 am, early by anyone's standards! It's winter, cold and wet, but not raining.

I'm just getting into a car with two friends who also enjoy the hobby of Urbexing.

Now, this hobby combines photography skills with the rather exciting activity of entering derelict buildings and sites. To get pictures of what's left of the history and fabric of a particular historical building.

The rules?

"Take only pictures, leave only footprints." No stealing, breaking in or being "tooled up."

Most of these trips are just a walk on. Some sites require jumping over a fence and finding an unlocked door or a missing window for entry.

In and out, great pics that record history.

In this case, it was the headstocks at the old Clipstone Colliery site in Yorkshire. All being knocked down for re-development.

Local mining history is going to be lost. (as I write this book they are still there actually, must be some push to keep them as a symbol of coal mining, no bad thing!)

"Lloydy, did you make a plan from Google maps? Entry and exit points?"

"I did! I've seen a road that goes around the back of the site, and we can park there and then it's a 5-minute walk to the buildings." (military guy, I've got this.)

Off we go. we get to the site and take the single track road just past the front of the headstocks and follow that for about half a mile.

"Seems a long way around Lloydy? Considering we are at the front of the site?" (as we drive past).

"It's fine, this road on Google went a little way out then curves back in." (I hope I remembered correctly)

On no, the road is completely blocked off! Someone has put large concrete blocks in the way to seal it off as it was a back entrance to the site, so they don't want people going in by mistake.

"Hey guys, no worries, we can walk from here."

"I hope it's not far Lloydy; we need to get in and out while it's still dark."

Well, it turned into a 40-minute hike across rough terrain, with all our gear. We got there just as it was getting light, which isn't ideal as we wanted to get in and out unseen by locals who may not like or approve of our Urbexing adventures.

We completed the Urbex and went out of the site's front gate in broad daylight. No harm done apart from a few disapproving looks.

The point to this story? There is always an additional element to every project as you work through the development phases. This is the "unknown unknown" we talked about earlier.

Even with proper planning up front and understanding of all your "unknown" elements, changes will happen or arise, and it's always hard to predict them.

So what's the answer to being more efficient in the face of that constant change?

Incrementally improve and learn from every unknown or unexpected change that you face and overcome. Embed that learning in the team. Record it, track it, own it.

Reduce the amount of unknown with each and every project, reduce the chance that the change request that comes in from that client is something that you have never seen before.

Make all those changes that come in, "small bumps" in the road, not big hills.

Did the Urbex crew ask me to plan the next trip out? Yes! Of course, I couldn't have known the road was blocked. There is no blame when something like that happens.

What about the next Urbex outing?

Did they let me forget though? NO! Every time we went out it was:

"Hey Lloydy, I hope you've planned better this time we don't want a 3-hour walk and another 10 miles to get in!" (Andy chuckles)

"Errr, a bit of an exaggeration I reckon."

However, the incremental improvement to our outings, now incorporated a bit more research on a second potential entry/exit point, and any additional risk in doing that.

We wouldn't be doing a 40-minute hike through the rough again …

Thinking about the triangle, the side component that got disrupted from the original plan was time.

We had less time so the output was affected, which resulted in a lower quality and effective Urbex. Less time to take pictures, having to go out of the front of the site.

We mentioned earlier that not managing your QA in the best way will lead to a crunch, managing change ineffectively and inefficiently will make that crunch even worse.

Failing to have a robust change management plan in place will very likely lead to a team's heaviest crunch periods.

Internal change management can be improved with good systems, and those will always help with the unexpected change that comes from an outside source.

This externally driven change is very hard to control but is always about all parties working together for a solution and often involves some level of compromise.

There is of course the change management of how the team in the studio responds to change, here's a great approach to help with that.

Learning Takeaway 10;

Planning will never be perfect, and there will always be an unknown or unexpected element, accept that. The key here is continual learning and increased capability within the team and its systems to reduce the power and effect of that element.

Making sure development is efficient enough through continuous incremental improvement, that way, when change comes, effectiveness is only disrupted in a small way.

Questions – Make Notes:

1. *Each team member needs to give an example where for them personally, an action or planned activity didn't go well, inside or outside of work.*
2. *What has each team member changed from that learning to make sure that same thing doesn't happen again?*

Understanding the DREC curve, to help with making change work.

This tool or technique has many names and is used in various ways; The Change Curve, The Bereavement Curve, and others, just Googling it will show you how many variations there are. It's rooted, I believe, in bereavement counselling.

How do people cope with that most challenging situation that is the loss of a family member?

The DREC part is an acronym for the four phases that pretty much everyone will go through with just about any change: denial, Resistance, Exploration, and Commitment.

From a work perspective, the key is understanding when each phase is active.

As someone moves through the change cycle, and generally when passing through Denial and Resistance initially, their performance can dip as they can actively push back on the change requirements and activity.

When we start to Explore the change requirements and try it out, performance picks up again, and by the time we are Committed to the change then our performance is often better than when we started because the original
 decision to make a change for improvement was valid.

A good example is when a particular piece of software is so embedded and used daily by the team; no one wants to let go of it.

It makes sense; it's worked for a long time, don't change what isn't broken right? Well if we don't explore new methods how would we ever improve?

So how do the phases of the DREC curve relate to this software? I think the conversation would go something like this, and it might be familiar!

"John, what do you think? Should we switch to the new software package that people are talking about?"

"Sally, I'm not sure really, why would it be better? What we use works perfectly well, the disruption would last many weeks, training, rollout, all the problems."

"Maybe' you're right, feels like a lot of work..."

Moving through the denial phase ...

Denial is the first hurdle with change management; John doesn't realise why, it probably hasn't been explained, there doesn't seem to be a plan, just that a change to the software will happen.

"Morning John, did you notice that the new piece of software we were talking about is being installed by the I.T. guys right now?"

"I know Sally! I can't believe it! They are just changing everything over!"

"I don't know how to use it, John, I'll have to do a bit extra to find out how it works."

"You know what Sally, I'm not happy about this, and I'm going to have a look and make a list of why it's not as good as what we already use, it will take me ages to learn it! I won't be able to get my work done. I'm going to ask I.T. to take it off my machine..."

So we enter resistance ...

John's performance will now drop, he's unhappy about the change, he's going to take time to discredit the new software, he's complaining to I.T. John is proactively working against the new software.

"Morning John, I was playing around and getting to know that new software last night, actually it was a bit easier than I expected and there's a couple of features our old software doesn't have.

I asked the I.T. team if they could give us a little training, and they said they would put together some videos showing how to use it."

"Really? I haven't looked at it yet Sally, I.T. have said they can't remove it."

"Ok ... if you reckon it's worth a look, then I'll give it a go when those videos are available but, if it's still not as good I'm not using it!"

Sally enters exploration and is taking John with her ...

Every member of the team, whether you are responding to the change or rolling it out will go through these phases of the DREC curve. It's just about how deep each person goes and how long it takes.

In this example John has a deeper and longer curve, Sally much shallower, she's getting to the exploration phase quicker.
Three months pass.

"John, I.T. is rolling out a new modular feature in the software package, I'm looking forward to seeing what it can do, some of the previous features over the last few months have saved me so much time!"

"Morning Sally, I can never get excited about I.T. rollouts, but I must admit, the new software has made things a bit easier for me, I wasn't sure at first, but this particular change seems to have worked."

Finally, we enter the commitment phase...

Everyone is moving towards commitment and getting there isn't always guaranteed, because every change isn't necessarily a success.

In fact, if people tend to keep pushing back and forth between resistance and exploration, the change initiative probably needs tweaking!

There are two really distinct benefits to the DREC curve:

1. When you see and place yourself at any particular phase of the DREC curve for any change that's happening, you suddenly become aware of how you are thinking, feeling and acting concerning that change.

   That will help you manage to move through those phases.

2. If some people are in resistance, it's either for a good reason or because they are hanging onto the old way. Then the change was probably, poorly planned, and not discussed with the team.

   People don't like to be in the dark, especially about changes!

As humans, we love our loops of familiarity, and we feel safe when we carry out activities that we know how to get through. Even the most radical people that love the spontaneous, the unknown, the adventure will have some activities, however small from which they don't deviate.

The DREC curve, along with proper change planning, and a solid reason why the change is happening, ideally with the whole team involved, will get to commitment much sooner than you think.

As we are going to be "change evangelists" to battle against the enemy that is the crunch, we need to understand how change can become easier within a studio.

Learning Takeaway 11;

The second critical part of managing change is understanding how the team will respond. Your planning and incremental knowledge improvement are critical, but if you can't deliver that change and make it achievable for the team then any efficiency it may bring could be lost. Worst still change itself becomes a problem. It only takes a few change management failures to end up with a culture block that fights it.

Questions – Make Notes:

1. *Discuss and make notes with the team about when a particular change went wrong in the studio and failed to get any traction. More importantly, identify why it went wrong.*
2. *With the same team take a change initiative that is currently happening within the studio and discuss where you all are on the DREC curve for that current change.*

It's time for us to go into battle with the crunch in every way!

We've spent the whole of Part 1 examining why development is challenging, what crunch is, why it happens, the effect it has on teams, people and projects.

We looked at two key pillars of development that are some of the biggest drivers of crunch, inadequate quality assurance, and change management.

The costs both in cash and outcomes, and when true crunch is present in studios, how it makes teams and leaders feel.

I hope we are all in agreement that software development without incorporating extended and damaging crunch, can only be a good thing?

Let's move on to Part 2, and begin to understand how to get to that all-important Zero Crunch position.

PART TWO:

Let's defeat crunch right now!

CHAPTER 7

Can it be only a 3-stage process to better development?

Rocket science? Well … not really, it's **incremental improvement.**
What you'll read in this part of the book should come as no surprise, there are many developers out there creating things, busy building what they are wanting to develop or being paid to deliver.

Every tool or technique I talk about in this part of the book may exist in some way out there in the world, but the critical component here is more about "why" and "how" you do it. You might play football, but that doesn't make you Cristiano Ronaldo.

Part 2 is about making you better at development whatever your level, to help you understand the power of people, systems and tools.

The main difference is that many methods and tools are used in isolation.

The right set of tools deployed in a systemised way, techniques for your people, data, project management, are essential, but they are only useful when layered with high-quality QA and fearless change management.

Why would you want to use my particular 3-Stage System? It has been built with over 20 years of experience in software and based on effective systems in the forces from decades of refinement, and utilised in studios to tremendous effect and the most crucial point?

You can use it too.

I'm not saying it's easy, there could be much to build, culture to understand, people to recruit to get to the right balance, but I guarantee if you follow these steps, then you will improve your development studio, whether you are a team member, manager or leader.

Why did I develop this 3-Stage System? We'll look at that next.

It's time to really "own" what you do and how you do it.

I learned many years ago when I was in the forces that what makes humans good at anything, starts with a feeling of accountability.

What I mean by that is when we choose to do any activity, task or action, whether work-based or just as part of our lives, there is a level of responsibility to something or someone that drives us to do it well.

Now, if that alone created a perfect approach to anything we do then why would I be writing a book about improvement? Many factors influence that feeling of accountability and drive the outcomes and quality of any individual or team performance.

Thinking back to joining the RAF (remembering that my reason was to get away from where I lived), I didn't know what I wanted to do or be within the service.

I turned up at the Tri-Service careers office, and I chose the RAF because I had an interest in aircraft (I had, as a child a cool book about the Space Shuttle).

Going through the process; tests, medicals, more tests, and the results ...

"So, Mr. Lloyd, we have your results." (Mr. Lloyd? I was sixteen!)

"Great! How did I do?"

"Very well on the technical tests actually." (Ok, that was a surprise as I didn't take technical drawing or metalwork at school, poor attendance meant those classes weren't for me - apparently)

"Ok, what does that mean?"

"It means, young man, you can pick whatever discipline you like in the engineering trades."

"Ok, so... what's the most interesting and pays the most?" (I thought I might as well earn what I could!)

"That will be, Trade Group 1, the aircraft trades; Airframes, Engines, Electrics, and Avionics."

"Ok, I'll go airframes please." (I was sixteen remember, I said "ok" a lot)

"Right then, let's get you all signed up for basic training, you'll report to RAF Swinderby in Lincoln for six weeks." (March 1984, at the tender age of 17 and one month!)

What followed was a crash course in discipline, teamwork, responsibility, (people and weapons), oh and more discipline for the 90 young men in my flight!

You've never seen such a shiny metal dustbin (yes dustbin), like the one I was polishing at 2 am after saying the wrong thing on parade!

After basic training there came trade training; basic and advanced engineering skills, aeronautics, principles of flight, mathematics, air systems, structure, you get the picture.

The learning was intense, structured and demanding all condensed into six months. Years later, what I realised was this;

1. The RAF instructors and system had assessed me, found my strengths and weaknesses in both capability and knowledge (my effectiveness).

2. They had then built me into a soldier first, then an aeronautical engineer, training for what I was learning, reinforcing where I had some knowledge,

and testing me to deliver the work where I was accountable. (efficiency)

3. Finally, they deployed me to be the best I could be in the real world, a capable engineer, team player, solid under pressure, able to respond to and manage change, and succeed.

I didn't start like that; I was as a young lad, 16-years-old with no idea of my capability.

The Royal Air Force put me through their tried and tested 3 stages of improvement. A system that made me feel accountable for the aircraft I fixed, the lives that were in my hands, and the team around me.

Responsible for doing the best job I could in any conditions.

Their system and mine have the same methodology but relevant to the software development industry.

Analyse – Systemise – Deliver.

This isn't about applying militant systemisation onto people, its about unlocking their potential so they can call on their capabilities in the harshest conditions.

Why military experience maps onto software development.

Those clients that spend enough time with me have probably heard me say.

"If I fixed the aircraft badly, then people could have died!"

Dramatic, I know, and people shouldn't (I hope!) die developing software, but it's clear that the point I'm making is about responsibility and accountability for our work. If the thought of a "blame culture" just came into your head, stop, now, that's not what I mean.

Blame culture is much more prevalent where there is a gap in knowledge and experience. Passing the accountability onto someone or something else.

Accountability is driven from the inside, "I am, and feel accountable," not "you are accountable." It should be used for good to stimulate activity, not weaponised to blame people.

I genuinely believe that a few key things motivate humans:

- Reward – in the form of responsibility, recognition, balance in their work and personal life and tangible rewards like money and items. (generally a combination and priority of these things at any one point in life)

- Knowledge – understanding what they are part of and why what they do is important and valuable.

- Progress to success – clearly working towards aims and goals, having an impact, and effect on something or someone.

There will be other, smaller motivators that are part of a whole, but I think those three are essential.

What is the opposite of that?

Poor reward systems, inadequate or incomplete knowledge and management of it, no idea what success looks like and how close we are to achieving it.

These are clear de-motivators in my mind for individuals and teams, and it is no surprise that;

These are ALL present during an extended crunch period!

When we are looking at individuals, teams or studios as a business to deliver projects out into the world, the 3-Stage System that has defined my working life for the last 35 years, through my military and engineering career and the last 20 years in software can be applied successfully.

It requires tailoring to any specific situation, but the core threads are the same; to get a team to the point where they embrace accountability and responsibility, are recognized and rewarded correctly for their efforts and understand why they do what they do.

That they are motivated by those natural feelings that push towards supporting other team members, rather than just money, delivering high-quality work every time and that studio systems not only support them to do that but create growth opportunities.

It's time to get the best out of the whole studio, to move towards success and away from survival, always being motivated away from failure and the constant stress of "feast or famine" development.

Let's break down the 3-Stage System into more precise actions, and understand why these actions will make a real difference to everything you do.

Measure twice and cut once, it's the only way.

This phrase may be familiar or entirely new, it originates from carpentry, making things, arguably one of the oldest work disciplines in the world. It merely means for everything you do make sure you double check before committing time, effort or money to the next action (in this case cutting the wood) as a mistake could cost you all of those things.

It seems that many companies in this world just cut, cut, cut! If they measure at all before acting, it's not a planned activity.

Stage 1 – Identify your pain, is all about measuring, knowing what you have and what you want before you make the change and act.

This phase is also about understanding why you need to make changes, you may feel they need to change, but fully understanding why has two key benefits:

- It will help the change to stick when you make it, the team will understand, they will have taken part in Stage 1.

- When you establish why, for this change, it often reinforces or informs the next one.

Remember, this is all about incremental improvement, small changes, continually improving as we go.
The studio and team meeting any change, challenge or activity that comes at it with a methodical and confident determination.

There are four activities involved in Stage 1 to uncover what you are good at and what needs improving or creating; Identify, Assess, Record and Change. We'll look at these in detail in Chapter 7.

I thought we already did all of those things, but I see now, there are gaps.

In Stage 2 – Build your systems, it's all about taking what we discovered in Stage 1, those changes that are needed, the gaps in our knowledge, systems, and activity and making them real.

Having the change support what the studio is doing and the team, but making sure we embed all this work within the culture, so it becomes part of what everyone does from this point on.

When the team embrace this kind of continual measure and improve culture what you move towards is a studio that understands what it needs to do to go forward and always be ready.

These systems support the team to help them be amazing, they don't hold any creative thinking back, whether it's for the development work or the studio structure.

The phrase "What if we" can strike fear into any team, when it comes at a time of crisis, the risk can be high. However, when used as part of the culture at any time, especially when there is no pressure, the thinking can be so much more fruitful.

"What if we build a way of making sure that code gets checked in game, now, before all the additional development kits arrive? We have the one kit to test it on."

Rather than?

"What if we just take a risk that the code will be fine, we are too far into a development cycle to be building checking processes, as we have had all those kits for many weeks, and there are other more important tasks to do."

For the first statement to be true, the teams need the time and the support to think this way. Being more effective and efficient at work will foster a continuous improvement style because the team will have already seen it successfully utilised.

In Chapter 8 some great tools and techniques will help studios and teams be better at what they do. This simple system using the results from Stage 1 is how you do it.

Create – Deploy – Improve

Then repeat!

Ahhh, now I see what the "secret sauce" that makes us great tastes like!

I've used the term secret sauce for years, I can't remember where I heard it. What we are talking about here is the "Colonel Sanders KFC recipe" for development studios.

Stage 3 – Master your business, is about understanding how to keep the studio and team in the No1 spot, running well and in demand.

Using business terms this is really two things:

- A Value Proposition for your customers – this is the ability to ease the pain that clients and publishers have when funding and delivering projects. You will become the go-to team and studio for the activities in which you are experts. (I know this because Rockstar Lincoln are exactly that.)

- Competitive Advantage for the studio – you are the go-to team because you are hard to replicate, not easily transferable and somewhat unique. In straightforward terms hard to replace and to find a studio as good.

Both Competitive Advantage and a strong Value Proposition will only come from being effective at what you do and efficient in how you do it.

You will be neither of those if you are over time or budget and have no (or weak) systems which cause crunch and damage the team. It's simple science.
The even better news?

When you have all of the above, then the economics of the studio and team look after themselves.

'You will make money and save money at the same time.'

The studio and team will be in demand, you already embrace change and don't fear it, you sign up to projects you can deliver on time and budget and you have robust systems that allow you to be flexible to meet requirements.

Best of all?

You will be ethical!! Your teams will be understood and rewarded fairly, new people will want to join, and the culture of incremental improvement means that embracing the 3-Stage System will be the ultimate "Crunch Buster."

Let others scrabble, have high turnover, lose knowledge and capability every day. You are part of a new way, that was born out of working the hardest crunch but learning why it isn't the way to succeed.

Let's have no more overpromising and under delivering through fear. You will, master software development.

Learning Takeaway 12;

Accountability is an essential feeling for anyone to deliver anything meaningfully. Coupled with responsibility, and both driven internally it is much harder to fail.
These feelings need to have supporting systems that embrace creativity in all areas and deliver learning. Managing change becomes a requirement to succeed

rather than a problem, and all of this represents a system of continuous improvement. Only a supportive culture will drive this activity.

Questions – Make Notes:

1. *Do you have a culture of continuous improvement? Identify and write down three examples of this happening. Post project is usually a time when this happens.*
2. *Do the teams operate on their sense of accountability and responsibility? Note down three examples of when you experienced that working and three instances of when it didn't.*

CHAPTER 8

Our worst enemy? Surely it's not us? Really?

Stage - 1, Identify your Pain.
In the last chapter, it was made clear and necessary to identify a starting point to get to better development practice and eradicate crunch.

It's one of those tricky things to do, to analyse how we work, to look in the mirror and assess our activity.

The thing is, there will be many activities that the studio and team are doing right, maybe even really well.

It's easy to focus on the bad things that happen, but it's more important to see how and where you are winning.

For the team to really succeed and be the best at everything they do, the knowledge within the studio needs to be readily available, of high quality and relevant to those that need it.

To get to that better place we need to think about these three areas of knowledge management as part of Stage 1.

- What knowledge do we have, and how incomplete is it?

- Where is our knowledge stored? Why and how is knowledge accessed and made available?

- What fundamental knowledge are we missing? What do we need to learn?

Keep these questions in mind as we explore knowledge management within the studio.

What do we know about anything and why? Let's build a shed and see.

Let's make a small but powerful distinction here, everything coming from me in this book has three dimensions to it when it's explained.

What, how and why something happens, or could be better.

Any other way makes the information somewhat incomplete for anyone using it. It's a critical point that whenever you are passing information to a team or within a studio that it's complete, and it doesn't matter if you are a team member, manager or leader.

Let's explore this using a non-development example so we have no bias at the moment.

This will trigger many examples in your own studios as we go through these sections.

It may be something we do as we get older and have a family, a house. There's nothing more satisfying than having a shed. (Maybe that's only me!)

Seriously though, unless you are a keen DIY nut, having built a thousand bits of IKEA furniture, or have a degree in carpentry, then you probably won't be able to do this.

Firstly, if I asked you what is needed to build a shed, then you could guess, roughly, these bits:

- Wood,
- Nails,
- Roof felt,
- A window, door,
- A solid base to put it on (concrete slabs?),
- Tools,
- Workforce,
- Time (the one that everyone forgets!)

If all these items (other than workforce and time) arrived on a lorry, were unloaded and piled in your garden, you may look at it all and get that little fear feeling start to build …

Just like managing all the unknown tasks you are given in a project.

So, we need the method, you know, how to put this shed together.

- Find a place for the foundation, lay it,
- Put down the shed floor.
- Start adding the walls and screwing it all together (with people, tools, time)
- Install the roof and felt it for waterproofing.
- Put in the window and the door.
- Everything is done!

When you step back, open a beer with your team, and admire the handiwork, what a handsome looking shed we've built! Strong, stable, watertight.

Then someone asks …

"Err, Lloydy, why did we just build that shed?"

The final piece of knowledge?

If you asked someone to do this task or help, and they don't know why, where is the motivation to make a well built, watertight, comfortable shed?

"Well, its a place for us to go and play video/ board games, make noise, and have fun! You and me! It's even got a drinks cooler and snack fridge."

The reason why is the exact reason someone will want to give it their best shot, which will always affect the quality of the outcome.

If we know, we are part of something important, and with a team doing it, then it matters.

I genuinely believe that one of the most significant problems in any development studio is not only where knowledge is stored, but that it is generally incomplete and fragmented.

Where's that information? It's never there just when I need it.

In many environments, and software development is no exception, I think there is a tendency to store knowledge that's out of date, fragmented, and spread throughout the whole business.

Some of it is in team members' heads, other bits are codified but incomplete, on a server, on a laptop on a piece of paper! So when people come to access and use the information they don't know how, or it's useless.

This leads to repeatedly filling in the gaps of how to use the information and why it's used, inefficiency is the only winner.

In many cases when this causes additional or redone work, human nature means we get defensive, and we start to impart blame, we begin to gather knowledge to protect ourselves for the next time it goes wrong.

I'm going to make a bold statement here.

One of the single most demotivating factors that a developer will experience is when their work is redone, firstly without consultation and secondly because it's seen as wrong or of low quality.

How do I know this? Because I've asked hundreds of interview candidates what demotivates them when delivering their work. That is the most common answer.

Many factors will contribute to this for that developer.

- The work brief wasn't detailed enough.
- The work that required innovation wasn't framed well enough.
- The Project Managers didn't see the direction I was going until it was too late.
- There is no time to let the developer rework within the schedule.
- Someone better (apparently) does the rework, but differently.
- The developer doesn't get told because there was no time.

The outcome? Damaged trust, frustration, a reduction in the desire to be innovative because "it will just get changed." These are seen as "people failures," the developer thinks the Lead failed them, the Lead thinks the developer failed them.

Well, this was a system failure, the developer couldn't access the right level and scope of knowledge to stay on track, and the Lead didn't have the time to make those briefs or the time to keep people on target.

There is no blame here, blame cultures are just bad news! It's a culture that will guarantee high staff turnover, unhappiness and ultimately poor performance in team members.

No, this is purely a knowledge management and communication problem. All these problems can be fixed.

We already have some useful information, let's check it, organise it and make it available to the right people.
In general, a good amount of data exists in the studio team, as an activity or experience that's currently not shared.

Time to change!

Learning Takeaway 13;

Incomplete knowledge sharing can be more damaging to the team and its output than having no shared knowledge at all. Within project management, loss of time through repeated work is widespread. The brief which is made up of; why, the knowledge, what and the method how to complete the task must be correct for all the tasks.

Especially important for those activities that are already familiar to the team. Which then allows additional time for the unknown and new work that doesn't have the full brief, to have the space it needs.

Questions – Make Notes:

1. *How do you communicate a change in the information and knowledge stored on the servers and systems? Make notes regarding the current system.*

2. How is the knowledge written and by whom? Do they understand the system and process to build and store knowledge for the team and studio?

No, all that knowledge can't just stay in your head.

It's very important that we "download" knowledge from within our heads, do you think that this vital experience is safe in there? I'm here to tell you it isn't. At best it's a bottleneck to activity, at worst it's lost.

It's perfectly reasonable for us to form and hold knowledge in our heads. As I'm writing this book, I'm effectively recalling and downloading all of my games industry experience so that I can give it to you.

When something good is created in the form of a technique or skill, method or action, in today's society it's seen as new or different, giving you an advantage.

Maybe it's that latest code module that shaves access time, or perhaps it's the recipe for the best brownies people will ever taste, it doesn't matter.

From a business viewpoint, this is important, and it's what helps you to survive, be different, excel, ensure success.

How about it? Shall we wholeheartedly agree that the information that's in your (or anyone's) head shouldn't stay there, it needs to be codified (written down) in a useful way and be accessible to all those that need it?

If we are to build a great team, great project and in the right way for software development, let's manage our knowledge in a better way.

On a side note, there's one important observation to be made here. The saying "knowledge is power" is a very heavily used business term.
There are certain sectors (legal, some sales, and others) where that is the simple mantra because the aim is to ascend beyond the person next to you, even within a company, at any cost, to deploy that knowledge to devastating effect. I know this, as I have a couple of friends that left Law to be developers.

However, this is software development. Look how much information out there is "open source." Many companies that start open source are hugely successful from having shared.

I'm not saying your development team or work should specifically use this method, what I am saying is that keeping knowledge as an individual within an organisation, or as someone managing a team is not as powerful as sharing good experience and the whole team using it to be better.

Real teams share the essential collective knowledge, and their performance is measured on their ability to use and deploy their work because of it. Remember the psychological contract? Trust amongst the team, respect?

The worst kind of knowledge management and holding it for sole benefit happens when a team has a blame culture in place, usually for the same reasons we looked at in the last section.

If you find yourself having to hold onto your methods and knowledge within a particular team to survive, it may well be time for a job re-think …

Now that we are starting to embed this feeling and desire to share knowledge. We need to know how to do it well!

Why incomplete knowledge is dangerous and destroys trust.

When information is accessed by those that need it to be good at their jobs, and it's not of high quality, out of date or fragmented, then it loses all trust. When this happens, the whole team start to believe that all the information that exists in the studio, on servers, or otherwise is weak and useless.

Worst still, that becomes the norm or measure in terms of people downloading from their heads and codifying it. A "that will do" approach.

Have you ever asked a developer to help with a job description? Well, what you generally get is a few generic, rushed lines of text.

If you ask them why they'll likely say.

"I'm no HR expert, and it's not really my job, I'm busy coding and have too much to do."

In fairness that is 80% correct!

However, what if your approach was?

*"Ok, but, what if the reason **why** I have asked you is that the candidate we want has to have the skills to support you and the rest of the team so that we can be more efficient? I value your opinion."*

*"**What** we need to do is have a robust and tailored recruitment process for this new coder, so we can save time and get the right person from a good job and person specification, get them in, trained and working effectively, and quickly."*

*"I know you aren't responsible for recruitment, but your input is valuable as you will have to work with this new coder. So there is an easy template on the server that asks simple questions to guide you **how** to help us build an effective job and person specification, so we are on the right track right away."*

This means there are two potential outcomes for recruitment in the studio:

1. **The way I see most doing it** - We recruit like every other studio, slowly, candidate after candidate, the time taken sifting through CV's and tech tests. Then we aren't sure if we got the right person, they might leave in a few months.

2. **The better way** - We have a system that identifies the gap in the team, what skills we need, who needs to be involved in deciding. We gather the information and narrow the requirement. We select CV's and interview only the good fit candidates, we only test those few, and we get someone who is a long term fit by having a proper induction and trial period.

There's a greater chance that those that helped recruit and select the new team member may be a little more committed to seeing them succeed and settle in better. Actually, this is a fact …

This recruitment example is a blending of Stage 1 and Stage 2 of this system; identify a gap in efficiency and effectiveness, gather the knowledge, and then build a system.

This system will save money and time, both precious commodities in the studio.

Learning Takeaway 14;

Knowledge within the business is the most critical component after team capability. It needs to be codified, complete and accessible for those that need it. When used by the team collectively it has the power to give an advantage to the whole studio. When kept by individuals, it can drive inefficiencies and actually reinforce a blame culture which at its centre, is destructive to teams.

Questions – Make Notes:

1. *Who are the people in the team or studio that have the most knowledge? Is it codified? Is it up to date? Spend time with the team and identify the gaps.*
2. *Do you feel there is a blame culture within the studio or team? Write down what you think are the symptoms and evidence.*

What don't we know? Should we find out?

Now we know what makes knowledge complete, how to store it, make it accessible and why we should codify it by removing it from the team's big brain's, we can start to look at the next part which is learning.

Most developers, managers, leaders, and studios, know what they are good at, their specialisms, their strengths, but what about what they don't know?

More precisely, what's missing from our "toolbox" of capability?

It's impossible to know everything, but it's not impossible to be good at everything you do, that's a choice.

The final piece of the puzzle is understanding what you don't know after assessing all the knowledge and information that's moving around a team and studio.

Simply put, any new and relevant learning that adds value to the project, the systems or any future activity is worthy.

Let's explore worthy a little more closely.

There's a saying that's used and accredited to many, Henry Ford, Albert Einstein, Tony Robbins.

"If you always do what you've always done you'll always get what you've always got."

There are problems with this information (using our new found information management skills!);

Firstly, there is no obvious provenance, if you Google this quote, various people have used it, rewritten it, said it incorrectly. One site states it's only from the1980's which would be after most of the people that are supposed to have mentioned it first.

What we have here is misinformation; when this comes into a studio, it creates chaos.

It doesn't matter that it's actually a great message, it really is, it's true, but if each person has a different viewpoint on what it means, or has found a modified version of it, then who's right? What's the correct answer?

We need to be more objective in selecting our learning sources.

A better quote for me is:

"Every day is a learning day". (Winston Marshall – British Musician.)

The message is simple and clear; the reason why it makes sense is apparent too.

The one rule when the team undertakes any learning?

"Additional training and knowledge collection that happens needs to be of a quality level that means it works for the studio, rather than being incomplete, out of date or incorrect."

With any specific training that will help fill a gap in a studio's knowledge, it needs to have value both for the person learning it and for the studio.

Ask questions about the quality, the consistency, the range, the delivery method.

Learning Takeaway 15;

When you identify a need to learn within the team or studio; a gap in its capability, it's vital not to let it become part of the same information chaos that may already exist. It will cost money and could become just another piece of mistrusted or non-adopted data on a studios server. All learning needs structure, value for all and come from an established and confirmed source. Poor quality and misinformation will create a situation that will only perpetuate crunch through re-work.

Questions – Make Notes:

1. *What learning systems are in place in the studio for individuals and the studio as a whole? Explore what you think is missing.*
2. *Create a list, that's also driven by the team of both the immediate areas of learning needed and those that would be great for the future. As always, the reason why is important.*

CHAPTER 9

Rome wasn't built in a day, so why would your systems?

S tage - 2, Build your Systems.
Having a vision for the studio and the team of what a fully working, supportive and effective system is, can be a great driver and motivator to get it in place.

The whole team needs to be involved, and it's essential when asking for a change, that it gets traction with everyone that it affects. Policy and system change is hard to "enforce" so don't try.

There are a few occasions when change needs enforcement, team and data security and safety being the main ones.

If someone in the team asks why the changes need to happen, it's not only that we should be able to say why, but that we believe in the transition.

That question is also a reliable indicator that any particular person probably wasn't involved in the previous discussion about any change that would be made.

Once we have identified the gaps in our systems and the learning required we need to build it within and for the studio. Putting these new processes in place is managing a change like any other.

There are four areas that our new improved systems need to embrace:

- Policy, Process, and Procedure; why they make us great.
- Supporting systems; why they will get you through challenging times.
- Real teams; why having the right people for the job is crucial.
- Quality; why it's essential and required internally and externally.

'How I learned to understand complexity, break it down and systemise it.'

One thing that has always been clear to me is that the best way to construct anything is to know all the parts needed.

There's nothing more certain to send a developer all glazed over and switched off than using the words ...

"System, process, policy..."

Worse still;

"Manual, operations, security..."

They'll leave the room if I say;

"Business continuity…"

I get it; you're creative, you make things, amazing things, you make fun, that's hard! (well unless it's Microsoft "no fun" Windows, just kidding Bill!)

Here's a different way of explaining how this all works, without the "business speak," the bits that are feeling like someone else's problem to deal with, you are a developer after all.

If you actually did what I'm going to describe at home, you can test the theory, as an engineer, I know this works.

The studio resembles a clay and wire construct.

Here's an analogy for you.

We are modelling clay, the substance that's the staple of any Potter. A slightly soft moldable clay that can be shaped into whatever we want. The kind of thing used to make mugs and plates.

We take a big lump, about the size of our fist, and we start making it into a ball, rolling it, shaping it. Takes a little while to get it just right, it's pretty much round now and finished.

What happens then is we pick it up, stand up and drop it?

The clay ball hits the floor, "thud." We pick it up, examine it, and the ball is no longer round, it has a big flat spot on it. It's pretty badly damaged, but we can fix it. We roll it and manipulate the ball, and after a good while, it's round again.

What we know is that every time we drop it, or throw it, or put something on it, the shape changes dramatically, because really, the clay is soft, too soft.

How can we make it stronger?

Get some wire mesh, chicken wire, so called as it keeps chickens in their runs. You've seen it, the thin wire that's in a grid that's easy to bend and shape. My whole garden fence is covered in this mesh, so that Dudley, my dog can't escape. It's the Jack Russell in him!

We cut some chicken wire, and we start to make that into a ball, we make sure it's got wire all the way through the middle, so that it doesn't easily collapse.

The thing is, I can drop the wire ball, throw it, and it bounces, but if I step on it or crush it with my hand, it collapses entirely. It's a bit too light and fragile.

You have two parts to the construct now but distinctly separate with different strengths and weaknesses.

So, we break our clay ball down into bits, that part is significant, then we start to push it into the wire ball, making sure all of the middle is filled with clay and the whole ball is now entirely made of wire and clay.

When we throw it at the wall, it still dents a little, but not nearly as much, it's easy to reshape as a ball. It doesn't crush easily either, the density of the clay supporting the ball with the structure of the wire. It has weight and effect.

It's still able to grow as needed, we can add more wire, more clay, and we know that we are building layer by layer on what is already strong. Equally, layers can be stripped away, without destroying the whole thing.

From the point of view of studio development?
The clay is your team; durable, flexible, capable.
The wire is your system; process, policy, and procedure.

Throwing the ball, dropping it, crushing it, represents change hitting the studio and team, and how it responds. The wire and the clay individually and separately take more damage when change happens. There's no point having systems if they aren't embedded in the team.

Together, the systems running through the team, the fact that they understand and embrace those systems, see them as support when change or challenge comes, makes them strong.

Stage 2 is taking the team, the clay, and threading all that knowledge we found and improved in Stage 1 through it just like the wire, reinforcing it, making it robust to unseen and unexpected change.

Finally, once the teams are entirely on board with the systems, and they create them too, as part of their work, it's like putting that wire supported clay ball into a kiln and giving it the hardest shell it can have, baking it in.

At that point, your ball will smash anything it hits, and anything that's thrown at it, with any damage being smaller cracks that can be easily repaired (incremental improvement). It's simple engineering and physics. To grow, just add to that strong foundation, and re-bake.

If you don't have a real team, and the systems and structure aren't there, then really it's just some small lumps of clay on the table. It's just the starting point.

It's time to review and build, create the systems and rebuild the whole studio in a stronger and more capable way. Whether it's to make the studio better, or before growing, this is an excellent way to make sure you have both stability and sustainability.

Learning Takeaway 16;

It can be tough to visualise what systems and structure are needed to support the team from the beginning. However, this is about incremental improvement too, which means adding information here and there as learning from success or failure happens to the team and studio.

If these small changes aren't made, then it becomes a huge task to rebuild the whole system for the team, as what exists is far too out of date and not trusted as a start point.

The additional benefit of these small changes is that the systems are then truly tailored and support the particular vision and direction of any studio or team. One size rarely fits all.

Questions – Make Notes:

1. *Please take a look at the systems that work in the studio and team, make notes why they work, and what they are made up of in terms of information.*
2. *Take any systems that are old, out of date and ineffective and bring them up to the same standard as the ones that work. Discard those that are no longer needed.*

Time to call the A-Team!

Yes, if you've been around as long as I have, you know I'm referring to the actual "A-Team"; Hannibal, BA and the crew from the (super cheesy) 70's TV show.

How does it go?

"If you have a problem and if no one else can help, and if you can find them, maybe you can hire, the A-Team."

I don't know how they did it, just with their skills, a few tools, a few bits of scrap and a massive dose of luck, all wrapped up in Hannibal's "I have a plan," was how they managed change.

'Success!' The good guys win, the bad guys lose, and all is well in the world.

The serious point here though?

They all had specialism (ex-Special Forces, apparently).

Hannibal was the planner and leader, BA was the mechanic and muscle, Face was the con man and player, Murdock was the pilot.

The A-Team are matched to the job at hand.

When change comes from any angle, internally or externally, at that moment the "A-Team" within the studio for that particular change request needs to be brought together and given the work.

In my humble opinion, the worst way to handle change is to try and slide it into the project schedule with everything else, you know to insert it in here and there, break it down into additional bits of work and then add those bits to peoples' workload.

What you end up with, if it all gets done at all, as the team is already busy, is half-done disjointed bits.

Get the A-team together, add it to the schedule as a chunk of work, and move tasks around to make it fit.

"Easy for you to say!" (I hear you yell …)

Yes, because when that change request landed, you carried out a process that meant that it was fully explored, understood, and the time and resource tweaked accordingly, right?

The triangle? You remember? You negotiated at the point the change came up to find the compromise to deliver it.

"But what if I didn't manage to get extra time? Extra people?"

Then the ONLY way for you to get that change done quickly and efficiently is by deploying the "A-Team," your particular version of it, for that specific change, i.e. the best guys for that job.

Within most studios, there is usually enough people to have many "A-Team's" for the different areas of software development. The key is identifying these.

I'm working with a studio right now; Hyper Luminal Games in Dundee, that has less than ten people in it, but their leader Stuart fully understands that people, when needed, can be multi-functional and be part of an "A-team" as required. In actual fact it's probably what has made Stuart and the team at HLG in demand and successful for the last 5 years.

Part of the success of working this way is that it means that a number (if not all) of the people in your team will have some knowledge of other people's work. (we'll talk about 80/20 next) This knowledge overlap not only brings contingency, but it's generally more exciting and somewhat empowering for team members.

When deployed it can also be a welcome distraction from their work, mainly if it's currently a grind or somewhat repetitive.

Learning Takeaway 17;

Absorbing and spreading the specific tasks arising from an unexpected change request rarely has the desired effect.

It removes the urgency which is the reason the change request happened. Having small and capable specialist teams in amongst the broader development team has an excellent effect on both efficiency and morale. Team members will appreciate the call to be part of the team, and a break from their normal routine.

Be warned though; this is about getting together the right people for a particular job or task, finishing it quickly and then going back to the usual routines. One is not at the expense of the other.

Questions – Make Notes:

1. *Is there a change management process within the studio for projects? Explore and discuss with the team how effective it is.*
2. *If there is one in place, using the information from question 1, make it better. If not map a new change management process out with the team and deploy it as soon as possible*

The 80/20 rule, reshaped to our benefit.

This split is used in many ways by many people, and I believe the original rule has this definition.

"The Pareto principle (also known as the 80/20 rule, the law of the vital few, or the principle of factor sparsity) states that, for many events, roughly 80% of the effects come from 20% of the causes."

If the knowledge in your studio follows the 80/20 rule in its purest form, then I'm going to go out on a limb here and say you are inefficient!

This inefficiency is directly related to the section about knowledge in people's head; it needs to be out, written down and shared with the team.

I'm not talking about everything, especially sensitive data; we don't want the team having information overload, that is the enemy of efficiency, look in your email inbox.

Information needs to be timely (at the right moment), relevant (hitting the right people) and accurate (concise and correct).

If we are to have "A-teams," if we can be flexible and respond effectively to change, then I recommend we flip the 80/20 rule for the teams' knowledge.

Instead of 20 percent of the team holding 80 percent of the knowledge (usually seniors and leads), let's make all our team members not only be specialists in their specific disciplines but have 20 percent knowledge of another subject.

Let me give you an example:

Many designers I know are multi-skilled, mostly design, but they understand some coding activity.

Now I can hear all the coders out there, reading this, saying ...

"No!! I'll end up re-writing that code because it will be poor!"

I hear you, but just for a moment, I'll have you consider that you are thinking about your work as an individual, really you are. What you'll have to do, assuming their work will be poor, probably having done some rework before.

What I will say is the 20% that this designer can do isn't across the whole of coding, it's a focused capability, a piece of knowledge that sits right at the edge of what they deliver.
Something that the team knows about that a Lead has helped to train in, that can be deployed if it's needed.

The Lead could be you.

The other effect is that as an individual, the designer will probably feel great about being able to work alongside their discipline but just on the edge. Still safe, and knowing that additional code knowledge helps them be a better designer.

So tell me coders, how many designers don't know how hard it is to code their designs?

Maybe this overlap will help a little with that awareness of how hard your job is.

We aren't just a circle of people, stood shoulder to shoulder, we have linked arms, that knowledge overlap makes us strong, understanding and supportive of each other's work and the challenge to deliver it.

Where there is a very active overlap is in production and all the other disciplines, production is the glue in amongst everyone that keeps things going.

Encouraging and building leadership skills in those that want it (don't force it!) will save the team more times than we can count.

If you are in a larger studio, this overlap may not need to be the case, and you can cherry-pick an "A-team" because you have a 100 strong group, specialists only. Fine, but what happens when that wider team is split into project-specific groups?

For small development teams, let's say five up to thirty, I think this is a critical skills balance. Without some level of overlap (knowledge and awareness) within those smaller teams, much of the change management and response will still be challenging.

Adopting this idea of 20% additional knowledge on the periphery of a skill set will help to prevent those dreaded questions, ones like:

"Can't we just - and add that in?"

Or,

"Can't we just - and make that work?"

Then developers have to come up with a different approach, adding to their workload, which not only takes time but is hugely stressful.

Crunch at this point is going to be the only option ....

Learning Takeaway 18;

Team members that own their work one hundred percent as their responsibility will benefit from additional knowledge that exists on the edge of their specialisms for two reasons.

Firstly, if that extra knowledge has the required quality and capability, then that gives a project great contingency when change happens.

Secondly, even if it's never actually utilised within a project, it creates an awareness when working with other members of the team when it comes to scheduling and delivery. Both of these are effective, but an additional side effect for team members is that it can be motivational too.

Questions – Make Notes:

1. *How many of the studio team has an understanding or capability overlap within their knowledge? Where would that be most useful? Which disciplines? Make a list.*
2. *Start planning in learning for the list you've made from question 1, whether courses or one-to-ones that build this knowledge and awareness.*

Quality and consistency is the only way, ask any famous coffee shop.

We've explored a few vital additional tools here to understand how to make the studio and team handle change in a better way but also spread further learning amongst the group, systemising inside the studio.

This quality component is both inward and more importantly outward facing.

Love or hate Starbucks, Costa or any coffee chain; they know how to deliver consistency and quality; they never quibble over replacing a bad coffee or push back on a customer.
Why? Because they know that 99% of the time what they do is right.

That's why people continue to go back. Starbucks has built a level of trust and delivery with their customers that makes them advocates; it becomes the proverbial "no brainer." Ask them where they go, they say Starbucks, and they probably tell others to go there too.

It's the same for development teams doing Work for Hire, and for those releasing their own I.P. Even the big publishers and studios need to understand this, if they don't then survival is in question.

Many things in life can make us comfortable as people, physical things; cars, clothes, houses, but this also extends to situations. What I mean is that loops of behaviour, surroundings, people that are like us, they all bring a familiarity.

We know how to order our favourite coffee in our coffee shop, where we normally like to sit, let's not talk about people taking "our" seats!

These are feelings of familiarity and consistency. We feel safe, and we know what we are going to get.

All these things apply to software development for clients and consumers, whether they are the game playing public or your publishing partner.
Shall we make a promise you and I, right now?

From this point forward, everything that any external party sees coming from the studio and team is of the highest quality, familiar in its delivery style and is exactly the work they are expecting.

This approach becomes a strong position for that fateful day when the studio doesn't hit a milestone or deadline because in this industry there are those that think:

"Well, you know, you are only as good as your last job, and that goes for making this mistake."

I call… NO.

Why? Because I know that after moving through the 3-Stage System, as a studio you are flexible, embrace change, deliver 99% of the time, there is familiarity and advocacy, and that there is no one else out there that can do this like you.

Just like Starbucks, you will fix this, and get you back to the "comfort position" expected.

Do you see Starbucks or Costa going out of business any time soon?

Then a studio's quality and service delivery when outward facing needs to be at it's best every time, even if some chaos management is happening inside the studio to assure delivery.

Learning Takeaway 19;

A culture of quality within a studio and team is a crucial component of the delivery inside on projects and outside for clients and consumers.

It drives the need to be consistent in how things are done, systems created, and learning and training are embedded. It adds an expectation for those working with the team and studio that when met will bring advocacy and support for what the studio is trying to do.

It helps both with negotiation for "Work for Hire" contracts, or to build trust when seeking funding for original I.P. It must flow through all of the methods that are in place to deliver projects successfully on time and budget.

Questions – Make Notes:

1. What quality measures, do you have in place within the studio for internal work and to manage external delivery and perception? Make a list and then discuss with the team the priority.

2. Build quality checking into the activity both internal and externally facing, using your priority list. Don't pick the biggest and most complex problem first; learn as you go.

This chapter has been about how you build in systems that incorporate all the knowledge management you need. How that's distributed throughout the team, but also how that can be called upon when needed to succeed and be effective in managing change and creating a culture within a studio and team that is cohesive and supportive of the aims and goals.

Chapter 8 looked directly at effectiveness and chapter 9 more at efficiency. The next chapter brings those two parts together and adds the all-important ethical and economic components of the business.

When you have started mastering all four to some degree, success is assured. Let's move onto that mastery in chapter 10.

CHAPTER 10

When you know what success looks like.

Stage - 3, Master your studio'
I've deliberately used the term "your studio" because you should be starting to feel accountable, part of a team irrespective of position or discipline and with a burning desire to improve!

Efficiency and effectiveness, less painful than I thought!

As you worked through chapters 8 and 9, reading the learning takeaways and planning actions based on them, it will have become evident that part of the mastery of the studio and its development process is comprehensive management of the knowledge needed by the whole team, coupled with tools to respond to change. You are creating efficiency in everything you do.

Making sure quality and learning run through the whole team will mean the studios' output is super effective, reducing the amount of repeat work, and the need to instigate change too many times.

The studio is better able to manage knowledge, change, quality, teamwork, and learning. Therefore, well on the way to being a studio that doesn't have to have a crunch culture.

The interesting side effect of this kind of positive activity is that any team will be much more motivated to work on the projects in the studio and even better, creativity will flow!

Confidence comes to the team that's hard to miss, a positive forward movement to overcome all the challenges that hit the studio. We can see this in team sports all of the time; a series of match wins, always brings new confidence, team spirit and collective desire to beat whatever is coming.

Studio teams can do the same thing.

Conversely, when the studio support systems are incomplete, inconsistent and low quality, teams can't depend on them. When this happens in sports (tactics, injury management, training sessions, equipment), the team will rarely perform as expected and certainly not at their best.

When you are part of something that feels like it could take on anything, humour, motivation, team spirit is high, that's certainly a place I would want to work!

Where does economy come into the equation, now we are back in control?

Stage – 3, mastering your studio has two other essential components, economy, and ethics. Financial stability can be one of the most challenging and stressful parts of studio operations. Economy covers all the activities that happen because every action has a cash cost to it.

Costs for all the wages, equipment, software and time. Just keeping the lights on in the studio (overheads), not to mention business costs like tax.

When the studio is running effectively, and efficiently then costs are controlled, reduced and managed.

Crunch will always cost more money; when the team is working beyond its maximum to deliver on tasks to meet a deadline, this unbalances the project management triangle (remember, the one that's resource vs. time vs. output).

Any additional resource, people and equipment, will be extra spend that wasn't in the specification at the beginning of the project. It may not be part of a change request where time and resource can or has been negotiated.

So, from where would this money come? Can you get it at short notice? (crunch is generally put in place at short notice). Will you have to withhold wages?

Did you miss that last milestone and therefore it's payment to fund the studio and team?

If you get through that crunch and meet the deadlines for the project, can you still keep all those additional team members in work? Let them go, and your reputation could be damaged for the next recruitment drive. Alternatively, they may have been costly contractors.

This "throwing money at the problem" type of approach is a downward spiral; it's HARD to get back from this point!

It all feels like panic, and you must have felt that if you've been through a crunch to deliver to a deadline, everything just feels out of control …

We are starting to get into the realm of ethics now as well as economy, let's look at both these areas in the next few sections as part of Stage 3.

The fear of spending and the measurement by cost, of people and the studio environment.

Budgeting can be as easy or as hard as anyone makes it. For most studios, this broadly fits into three categories, cost of people (time), studio space and equipment.

It doesn't matter if you are a full-blown independent or managing a budget in a studio funded by a publisher. It's money in and money out.

There needs to be balance across this spending, but in reality, without the right people, rewarded the right way (fair pay is one of those rewards), there is only an office space with equipment in it and zero creativity or activity. So let's agree that the lion's share of the budget needs to be on the team.

I've always been a music fan, listening to records and tapes in my earlier years and recently CD's and streaming services. To get the best "sound for your Pound" (or Dollar!), there was always a recognised budget split for your Hi-Fi equipment.

The split is 40 percent for the source, 30 percent for the amp and 30 percent for speakers.

The idea is that the source of the sound is the most important, but the route to our ears needs to be good enough to do the source justice: weak speakers, poor sound.

Balancing the budget for a development studio is more complicated, but it's not dissimilar in approach.

Imagine a studio where the team are paid fairly and well for what they deliver, in an office environment that's comfortable and fun, with additional activities that reward and motivate — using equipment that enables them to achieve their work in the best way and on time.

Sounds expensive? Well, that's the trouble with measuring everything by cash only. What I've described is perfectly scalable based on budget, team experience, and size, and equipment levels required. Every studio, project or task has a cost to it, and the planning before it all starts has that all-important cost element.

The mistake comes when there is a set budget for a particular project or Work for Hire piece, but when spending it, there's a continuous effort to save every penny on every purchase or hire. With recruitment, if you hire someone and manage to get them to agree to a salary that is the lowest the studio can pay them, that single fact will always be at the front of their minds when they are needed to go a little above and beyond.

There's no specific answer to accurate budgeting; an accountant will tell you budgeting is mostly "best guess," especially the farther out in time you are predicting.

Rather than giving you a set of guidelines around how to build a relevant budget, I want to provide you with a series of statements that need to be understood if you wish your budgeting to support project delivery.

- If you don't allocate some budget figure to all of your project activity up front when that particular cost comes up during delivery, it's likely it will feel like it's too expensive or you don't have the cash to cover it.
- A team never delivers on time and quality, with poor or under specified equipment.
- People's performance, when measured as cost per hour, e.g. "that 4 hours of creative thinking cost £200 and we ended up with nothing," rarely has a positive outcome. The work the team achieves will start becoming what can be directly proven, rather than delivery coupled with creativity.
- If the space that the team works in is both too small and uncomfortable, then the team over time will become demotivated and likely less creative, which could lead to underperformance, crunch and additional cost.
- Cash flow is required for every project, a contingency amount for any additional spending that might arise for previously unknown parts of the project, or when a change request forces it.

To be very clear, this isn't about palatial offices, high-end equipment, and the most significant salaries; those do have a place, but this is about relevance for the team and project delivery.

As a general rule the more experienced and capable the team, the higher the level of spend on the environment, but many industry veterans are attracted to an ethical culture within a business where they can really deliver for themselves and others.

Good examples of spending that supports a strong culture are those that "surprise and delight" team members — a well planned and enjoyable Christmas function, surprise event days, and fun activities.

At Rockstar Lincoln we introduced an on-site canteen. It enabled the staff to order breakfast for the following day, at cost (the cost of the ingredients). The kitchen team would prepare all the breakfasts and email the team members when it was ready, and they would go to the canteen to eat it.

This breakfast gathering had two benefits, as a young team, the chances are they wouldn't have had breakfast; this way they got something to eat that was easy to order and cheap.

The second benefit was team members getting together to eat it, discussion, interaction, and friendships.

For those that are thinking …

"But what about the productivity loss?"

Well, for the fifteen or so minutes it takes to eat breakfast and have a bit of fun and chat, the productivity and motivation back at a person's desk was much higher. People are not machines.

The studio spend initially was on the kitchen and canteen fit out, factored into the budget. However, then it became only the two kitchen staff and power. The cost was low, and the actual benefits were very high!

This section was more about an approach to budgeting rather than the specific detail of any area. If you follow those guidelines, then you have a better chance of keeping the team happier, the productivity up and the whole project on budget.

If the answer is yes to any budget to get the deal, then the whole venture may already be underfunded. That's why before saying yes, a full understanding of requirements, team capability, and delivery is the only way to go.

Remember, "buy cheap, buy twice."

Actually knowing our people, starts from moment one, or it's pretty much Russian Roulette.

When I initially engage with any studio to help them be better at what they do, the majority of the time the first pain they what me to help with is recruitment.

I think the most challenging part of recruitment is understanding who you need to fill the gap in the team. What I mean by who is not about the technical capability to do the work where the gap is, I'm talking about who the person needs to be to connect with the team, fit in with the culture and be motivated and happy.

If you are thinking that making a team member happy comes down the line when they have settled in, then we are already in trouble!

There's often a primary focus on the technical aspects of a role, after all, that's why a studio needs to recruit, a gap in knowledge, not enough of a particular skill, an overwhelming workload, that's certainly the way you generally filter applications.

The thing is when you have a shortlist (or sometimes a massive list) and the next phase of recruitment starts, generally, the focus will still be technical, tests and review.

Just think about the amount of time that has been spent assessing the CV's and then the tests for technical fit, other team members may have been involved, there could have been hours of work even before the first meeting. The candidates have also spent many hours with the technical test too, and it won't be great if they fail to get the job because of team fit.

It makes sense, that after the CV's have been filtered for a technical fit, that the next phase should be team fit.

The next step of the process should be an interview. In which both parties get to know each other, how the studio works, what the reward requirements for that particular candidates are. How the culture works, what motivates and demotivates?

This interview is the moment where you are discussing the first steps to long term happiness, learning and support because filling a role in the team on both counts is equally as important.

The one weakness in an interview is that it's usually relatively short, around one hour, the candidate and the interviewer could be a little nervous, the questions bland or generic, and the answers too simple. At the end of it, what do you know? What have you learned? Not much.

There are better ways to conduct interviews, all I'll say is, remember, you are the studio with the gap in its capability, you are the one with the need, and they are looking for somewhere to work, to fit in, to be settled and happy. Remember, this is aiming to be a joint and balanced relationship.

Many years ago (about fifteen as I write this), I started using psychometrics in my studio. I learned why it was valuable and when to use it. More importantly that it is candidate focused and not a stick to beat people. If it's a weapon at all, it's to understand people more.

I've been administering Psychometrics for clients for many years, and it's the single best tool to use to understand what the comfort zones and motivations and more importantly what the demotivation's are. This information is more critical when recruiting leaders and managers.

The main point here is that it's an accepted fact that people can and will only work and continue to be happy and motivated when they are pretty close to matching where they are comfortable based around personality.

A good example is assertiveness. (definition - having or showing a confident and forceful personality.)

Some people are naturally assertive and will drive their opinions and actions forward; others are less assertive and may not want to be. This behaviour is pretty typical in most teams, but generally, whichever you are you become pretty unhappy over time if you are continuously expected to work excessively in the opposite direction for an extended period.

Asking an assertive person not to have an opinion and making someone less assertive stand-up and give their idea in a room full of confident people is folly!

Why does happiness matter? Well in a transactional sense it doesn't (work for cash), but remember earlier in the book we talked about the psychological contract?

Ask yourself this, as a leader or a team member, if you are unhappy, how would you feel about having to step up for the team and do extra hours for a project sprint finish? Alternatively, how committed would you be to that additional learning that's not explicitly part of your role?

Psychometrics is a great tool to use to bring a bit of objectivity to the recruitment process. The candidate answers the questions according to their likes dislikes, motivations and demotivation's, and they are giving the information that helps you better assess what works for them to make sure that not only the new person fits with the team, but the team fit with them, and the culture of the studio.

It's neither good or bad in the way someone would answer a test, but when we get recruitment wrong, for both a candidate and the team, then it rarely ends well, and from both sides, there has been work and effort that may have been wasted and possibly family upheaval.

Learning Takeaway 20;

Happiness in a particular role and workplace has many components to it. The work, the people, the place, the pressure and the success, even the commute. These are all hard to understand and measure for either party when someone new joins a studio and team. Recruitment needs to explore that as much as possible if that new team member is to stay happy for the long term.

A combination of subjective and objective approaches within the recruitment process will help reduce that risk. Ignore this need and high failure rates with increased costs will be the outcome.

Questions – Make Notes:

1. *How much of your recruitment process focuses on the people fit rather than team fit? How subjective is the process, and how candidate focused rather than studio focused is it?*
2. *Discuss with the team, methods and ways recruitment could improve. Who would be involved in those changes and how.*

Are there any guarantees with team fit?

Are there guarantees with anything when talking about people? No, not really, but this is about reducing risk and laying the best foundation for any future and real team-based relationship.

The benefits of this type of approach are:

- A greater sense of fit from the first time the two parties meet.
- A more objective assessment for both parties.
- Additional information that can be used to tailor the induction and trial period to fit the style and personality of the new starter.
- A better chance that the new team member will be up to working speed quicker.
- A quicker and stronger socialisation with the team and the culture.
- A new team member that will likely share how things are going for them in the early stages.

The risk if this approach isn't adopted?

That good old ...

'Throw them in the deep end, with a sink or swim mentality.'

What happens then is discomfort, stress, a high chance of failure.

Worse still, team damage and unrest, demotivation.

I'm willing to bet that most of you reading this book have known a person in a team that just didn't fit.

It's generally not their fault! If they knew what they wanted and the studio did too, you wouldn't have employed them!

Is there a bad person out there you don't want in your team? How do you know?

I'm a big fan of "right person, right job" if a person's moral values are matched to society in general then they will likely fit in most roles.

Have you considered the possibility that it may be true that some personality types can be described as "not playing well with others?" This idea may prove unpopular with some of you reading right now, but it's counter-intuitive when thinking about a real team.

I know and am aware of many many amazing people in the games industry and software development generally. Working hard and making groundbreaking games and software.

However, there are those that will create problems in teams and unbalance the culture in the studio. Who knows the reasons why?

It's essential and a valid reward to be recognized for what we do, it's motivational, and often inspirational but when that recognition is consumed in a way that it's about "what I did" rather than "what we did," the empathy and accountability for the team can be missing.

During recruitment, a candidate leaning towards that personal requirement has to be matched very carefully.

Recruitment to match a stabilised culture within a studio is not easy, but in general, there is a good dose of emotional intelligence, empathy, and humility, and these are mainly required in leaders.

Please don't confuse this with drive, confidence, determination, and commitment, for me, all these are present and active in good team members and leaders too.

'Go-getters' (an aggressively enterprising person.) have a place in business, and its part of an entrepreneur's makeup. However, I would suggest in the case of the team it's about "never giving up" rather than "at any cost."

In my experience, real team players, irrespective of fame, fortune or level of success, will always use "we" more than "I."

There are many jobs, where a self-facing focus, for example great salespeople, TV show hosts, and PR guru's, and in recent times US Presidents is a requirement. But I would suggest that working as part of a creative team in the studio, would mean they'd be pretty unhappy when deeply positioned within a team on a daily basis.

Deployed to secure funds, build branding, or to blaze a trail, they will be incredibly powerful.

I'd like to think there is no such thing as a bad person, but as a studio, we have to know who we need and how they fit into our teams.

What is performance management and do we really need it?

When we are recruiting well, getting the right kind of people, motivated team players that want to thrive and create, how do we keep them happy and focused?

We reward them, give opportunities to grow, feel valued, recognized. In the book of HR, this falls under performance management. Not sure about you, but when I say this term, as I have to as a consultant, I get a little uncomfortable feeling in my stomach.

Not as uncomfortable as a phrase I heard once, "natural wastage," apparently describing people that would leave a job of their own volition or through retirement. (seriously, Google it, it's a real term)

So, let's leave these uncomfortable phrases behind for a moment and look at this from a different angle. Getting this far in the book means you are starting to fully understand the idea of why we do anything within the studio. I think that's obvious for this section but let's define it as

'Helping people to be the best they can be for both themselves. the team and the studio.'

It reads a little bit like a cliché, but to be frank, it's pretty much on the money.

In my experience many studios implement a system for performance management, this is effectively how they will carry it out, but it's going to be pretty ineffective if they don't know why and what it needs to be for their particular team and studio objectives. Here's an example.

John's thinking about this year's appraisal ….

It's that time of the year again, your Lead just mailed you the "what are your goals and objectives for the year?" document, as it's coming up to annual appraisals.

We do this exercise every year, and I'm not sure what to put in there! Is it even my job to set my own goals? Especially when I take the time to do it, but rarely is there time in the year to fulfill them.

Worst still is the appraisal interview. It just feels like we talk about what I did in the last month; no one really seems to see things I'm proud of. It's not the recognition I care about, but there are areas that I feel I've taken on more responsibility without even being asked.

I'd love some training in those areas; actually, I found it really motivating, and I know that my colleagues see the benefit too.

The Producer over at the publisher responded well to the changes I made about six months ago, and they want that to be the new way. I wonder if that's the kind of thing I should talk about at my appraisal? I'm just not sure, it's generally only a quick chat, essentially asking if everything ok, then any pay changes.

Here we go then.

"Hi John, come in! Sit down, well, it's that time of year again!"

"Thanks, Jason, yes, appraisals eh? They always make me a little nervous." (need reassurance to discuss what I'm really thinking)

"So John, people are telling me that you're doing an excellent job on that latest project, the one we started four weeks ago, well done."

"Ahh, ok, yes Jason, it's going well, although I've just started and I'm picking it up." (Really? I'm still learning that, not sure I'm doing a good job yet)

"Great! How's everything else going? Well?"

"Err yes, I think so, and we are getting through the tasks." (I think that's what he's asking about?)

"So, let's talk about cash, it's been a good year, so we are giving everyone 5%, good right?"

"Thanks, Jason, yes, that's very generous." (Everyone? Ok,)

"Great, I need to say, sorry that I haven't been able to read your whole goals and objectives doc, just snowed under. But you seem all over the work anyway John, as always."

"Right, ok, I'll just push on with those aims and objectives?" (The same thing happens every year, not sure why I bother filling it in.)

"Sure, you're a good guy, I trust you. Are there any other questions?" (As he scores through my name on his big list of people to see)

"No Jason, I think I'm good." (Sigh, I just didn't really get a chance, I know he's busy)

"Great! Same time next year! Thanks, John."

I'm pretty sure that as a team member or manager, you could have been on either side of this conversation, it may be all too familiar. It's hard for managers to know everything, but if there is no way of tracking the activity, no time to thoroughly discuss and set meaningful goals, it's just going through the motions.

This can be really demotivating for all parties.

For those being appraised, there needs to be bravery to ask, discuss and mention, so that the whole system and relationship can improve.

This is yet again a system failure rather than a people failure, and is the primary problem with performance management systems; One size does not fit all. A performance management system must be tailored to the studio.

Ok, so what do we need? Let's put some boundaries around this system and content inside it, i.e. what should it cover? What are the building blocks?

From a team and people perspective:

- Rewards – Recognition, responsibility, work/life balance, money.
- Growth – Learning, training, experience.
- Flexibility - culture, hours, non-work activity.
- Time – Interaction, understanding, support.

From a studio and activity perspective:

- Value Pillars – culture, beliefs, work ethic, team spirit.
- Capability – skillsets, credibility, dependability.
- Delivery – Quality, consistency, familiarity.
- Growth – stability, incremental improvement.

If this is already starting to feel complicated, that's because it is! Performance management is never easy to set up, but once set up it is easy to maintain when it's valued and embraced by the team rather than something that's applied to the team.

I'm not going to go into how to build this for any studio, and each is different. But I will say that much of the knowledge and activity in those two lists will actually already exist within any team or the studio.

It needs bringing together, analysing and then a consistent approach that works, is efficient and embraced by the team and forges the way to better performance management.

It sounds like performance management is a perfect candidate to put through Stage 1and 2!

Learning Takeaway 21;

A poorly implemented performance management system can do more damage than not having one at all.

The idea that managers can keep awareness of all the individual wins and successes as well as the failures or challenges in a team is flawed. Applying a "one size fits all" system is equally flawed, as those that it doesn't suit or fit will probably be highly demotivated by it.

A lighter and relevant touch, tailored to the team's culture and built around reward systems and a studio's value pillars has a greater chance of being adopted and useful to the team. As studios get bigger it's harder, but like project management, teams can be broken into smaller parts to enable a flexible and tailored approach.

.

Questions – Make Notes:

1. *Does your studio have a performance management system? Is it followed? Successful? What do the team think? Discuss it with them.*
2. *What parts of what exists, actually work? Working with the team to identify the studios value pillars, goals and objectives. Start building a system that supports those aims.*

Stage 3 is the most challenging to apply, as the job is never finished.

In this chapter, we have looked at the additional areas of economy and ethics that when coupled with efficiency and effectiveness are the cornerstones of successful software development and the cure to crunch.

I can't emphasise enough that people are at the core of any software development; they are the creativity and lifeblood.

Enable them to be great for themselves and the studio, with strong and supportive systems and the economy of the studio will look after itself.

In the last chapter of this book, we'll discuss what it feels like when software development is motivational, ethical and cost-effective.

CHAPTER 11

Did we just enjoy delivering a project, on time and budget?

Y ou now have the tools to remove real crunch from the studio.'
There will be industry and development veterans out there that have a different viewpoint regarding crunch and delivery.

I'd have you consider though that we can't just keep developing software in the same way as we move into the future. The burnout and destructive way crunch gets a project to its end is just not sustainable.

The reason I developed this "3-Stage System" is that there is a different and better way. I can live with the fact that traditionalists will develop software their way, I used to be one, so I understand.

I can live with the fact that I can help studios and developers finish projects on time and budget while traditionalists still crunch.

I can live with showing studios a more efficient and effective way to move through projects, while traditionalists scrabble continuously to finish. I can live with the idea that the whole team can have fun delivering projects, while traditionalists apply pressure, fear and blame to meet deadlines.

I can live with the fact that with this system a studio and its team can say no to a project because it can't be done or isn't right for the studio. While traditionalists, search and take as much business development work as they can and then try to work out how to deliver it.

Most of all I can live with the fact and feel proud that any studio and team that utilises the 3-Stage System in their particular way, are making their journey in software development a fun, comfortable and successful one.

There are a number of significant side effects of teamwork and development in this way, that only add strength and fortitude, giving us that bravery to take risks and not be reckless or driven by fear. To push the boundaries of what we know and develop, to continuously improve.

Firstly, I want to take one of the last cultural mistakes and remove it before we look at those beneficial effects.

Why blame culture never helps, it's simply a team smasher.

The desire to blame others has never been so prevalent in society as it is today. It's someone else's fault, it shouldn't have happened, and blame gets applied with some sanction or action.

This blame effect is powerful when we think back to the DREC (Denial, Resistance, Exploration, Commitment) curve for managing change, and it always happens in the resistance phase.

When we push back on a change, we blame either the person who wants to instigate it for our personal dip in performance or capability as the change happens.

That's pretty normal actually until we get to the exploration phase and we move beyond (or should) that blame, we don't hold onto it.

Applying blame likely comes from the desire to protect. Our survival instincts kick in, how do we defend ourselves, and by that, I mean income, family, safety? We push back, and we move the responsibility to others, the real perpetrators in our eyes.

Ok, let's add a good dose of crunch activity to that blame position we are taking …

It's Friday morning; three weeks from the final build.

"Simon, you said you could do that task in two days, and we are now three days in, and you haven't completed it, other people are waiting on your assets. You'll have to work through the whole weekend to get in front."

"Hold on a minute Nick, you asked me to give time estimates on this task weeks ago. Since then there has been so much scope change in this area and in the art assets, the job is much more complex now, it will take longer! You didn't adjust the schedule for the added complexity."

"I shouldn't have to adjust the schedule. If you had hit those previous two tasks on time last week, you wouldn't be so far behind."

"That's not fair Nick, and you know it isn't, I picked up a couple of extra tasks that weren't in my schedule because Julie was ill and had to have a day off sick, this is so unfair, I had plans with my family this weekend."

"Sorry Simon, but that's the way it is, you know what the publisher is like, we can't miss that date, we won't get paid if we do.

"It was the publisher who requested all those changes that have put us behind! You should manage that Nick, that's your responsibility! I'll work the weekend, but I'm not happy, and my family won't be either ...."

This scenario will be all too familiar for those of you that crunch. But who is to blame? Nick, Simon, Julie, the publisher even Nick's family?

That's the point. Everyone could blame everyone else, but where is the win? Where is the solution going to come from amongst all this fighting? There are definite system challenges in this example around scheduling, manpower, change management, but no one is thinking about solutions, just deciding who's fault it is, applying blame and pushing back.

Crunch is like throwing fuel on the fire, and it helps a blame culture burn very brightly!

Blame removes any desire to take risks, it's not about repair or overcoming adversity and then move on to the next challenge, it's about the wrong kind of analysis, measuring the people rather than the problem itself and overcoming that. Yes, we need the right people, but if time after time blame is apportioned for mistakes or challenges, then it's like a team actually punching itself in the face.

What's the opposite of blame culture when challenged?

There is a way and it goes like this.

What happens when we are in the mud, and the bullets are flying?

It's just a whole lot better together! I remember one particular feeling from both my time in the military and studios at Rockstar and Activision.

The relief I felt when I had others with me to tackle a big problem head-on. It's not to say that I didn't have to do things on my own, we all have to face personal fears and overcome tragedy and adversity. But doesn't it feel so much better when you do it with others?

I'm going to bet that at some point in your life you got into trouble for something, at home, school, work? Taking school as an example, if you got into trouble it was infinitely easier to process, manage and get through when someone else was in trouble with you.

It didn't matter if they were friend or foe! It just felt easier.

In some cases, if it was your foe (let's say it was a fight), the action of being in trouble together may create a bond between you. Suddenly you have a common challenge to tackle, together.

So empathy kicks in, understanding, you may even apologise to each other before you both see the Headmaster. It's a tribal thing!

These feelings are no different in adult life, the activity that is helping each other to overcome diversity is I believe, genetic.

In it's most intuitive and challenging application we see whole countries go to war for their countrymen whom they don't even know, but have a collective sense of responsibility to protect and defend.

Bringing this back to software development, projects and teams, we can identify times and situations where it feels like we are "all in it together," and how overcoming those challenges can make us stronger than ever.

The actual sprint finish, when overtime isn't crunching.

Very early in the book I mentioned that not all overtime is a crunch, I want to explain that idea further as there is a clear distinction between soul destroying crunch and the learning and team bonding that comes from overcoming adversity as we've just discussed.

A number of Studio Head's and CEO's believe the same. Marc over at Tag games in Dundee suggests his idea of overtime versus crunch as;

"No one should put their health before the completion of a video game, but also the team pulling an extra hour or two for two weeks isn't going to do that.

Personally I think if it's more than a month of extended work hours, where the team are needing to be fed in the studio, you could call that crunch."

We mentioned accountability from within in a previous chapter, this idea that we are responsible for our piece and part of the development creation and process. We are all in agreement that it's hard to be creative when faced with deadlines.

I don't know about you, but when I've agreed to be part of something or do my bit, the responsibility I have to the team and the project is the primary driver.

When the team is very close, that adds another layer of desire to finish and finish well. In my experience, this is where the greatest satisfaction and achievement comes from, with the recognition that the whole project and the people that created it made something amazing.

Harness that power to deliver and any overtime becomes part of getting that project completed, not enforced, extended and damaging crunch.

Everyone sprints towards the finish, together!

Stability followed by the unknown challenge and then a win, rinse and repeat.

It's all about confidence. But, what is confidence?

"The quality of being certain of your abilities or of having trust in people, plans, or the future." (Cambridge English Dictionary).

In team sports, this confidence comes from a series of wins; whether it's football, rugby, cricket, netball, hockey it doesn't matter, it really doesn't. If a team are on form they are almost unstoppable.

They train and practice, learn to predict each other's actions, know each other's strengths and weaknesses, support each other. The coach has a game plan for any particular opponent, taking on a match that's slightly different. This is a pretty unknown element, but with at least some knowledge of how the opposing team will play.

If the team wins its next match (you, should be thinking projects now, delivering on time and budget), the next training session builds on the strengths that helped the team win.

If the team loses that match, the next training session focuses on where the gaps were, filling those with knowledge and capability. There might even be additional training to master the new tactics. (overtime?)

The core actions here?

- Analysis from every match.
- Learning why it was a win or a loss.

- Deploying the learning.
- Incrementally improving.
- Working as a team to overcome.

As a software development team, this confidence-building activity will help you deliver projects that are increasingly complex or challenging.

With known stability in the early development phases of a project, and a dose of chaos management to overcome the unknown to get to the finish line. Where creativity is smashing against deadlines but incremental improvement is the post project mantra, we are unstoppable!

Deliver on time and budget most of the time, and your studio's confidence will be hard to deny.

Bring on the next one!

Master each battle and you might just win the war!

Except for blame culture, as that needs cutting out of a studio, those more excellent side effects we've just explored; in it together, and confidence to master a sprint finish, are team specific, but what about the system based ones?

Well, when a studio has better systems generally the singularly most powerful side effect that comes from effective planning as part of the 3-Stage System, is being prepared!

There's a saying that revolves around goal setting.

'How do you eat an elephant? One bite at a time.'

Now, I'm not suggesting you do, as Elephants are amazing creatures of course, but you get the point?
When faced with a massive objective that seems overwhelming, we need to break it down into manageable chunks (individual goals). Sounds obvious? So why do so many projects go over time and budget?

Because without the 3-Stage System preparation it's nothing more than best guess, assumption, and hope.

When you plan in a better way, it's unimportant how big the final required outcome is, as long as it's broken down into manageable parts of delivery in any project. It really is just a larger Project Management triangle with more time and resource to get there.

You could be digging a hole, building a bridge or making a video game, it's the same idea.

But consider this, if you have that overview of delivery of all those key milestones and deadlines (the smaller chunks), the "A-Teams" are ready to go, the whole team is multi-skilled (80/20 rule), motivated and confident.

There are very few gaps in the knowledge (efficiency) of how to do this, all the tools are available to the team (effectiveness), the unknown elements have been explored and given the creative space they need.

Boom!

Your systemization has prepared you for each battle, each change that comes in, and delivering those unknown, new and unusual parts of the project, that make it unique.

You are prepared, ready, and you … will … win!

That feeling of achievement, both as individuals and as a team, you can't beat it.

Those that have known me a little while have probably heard me mention "smile moments."

For me, these moments are what make life a joy, without them it's just a hard road, and it doesn't matter how challenging or difficult a situation people find themselves in, these smile moments can and will happen.

Let me explain.

All of us had a moment in the last few minutes, hours or days, where you were doing or saying something, part of an activity or watching others when you suddenly realised you had a big grin on your face!

That's the key though, it's not making yourself smile, it's being unaware until you are aware that you're laughing.

This comes from a sense of satisfaction, pleasure, and enjoyment that happens on the inside, it triggers, and you feel great.

Examples for me are many, but here are a couple;

I'm a self-confessed petrol head, motorbikes, and cars, and for me, a massive, yes massive grin comes across my face, and I can't help it or stop it, I don't want to when I hit the accelerator of a car and hear the roar of a V8 engine!

Sat here, writing this page and thinking about it is making me grin right now because I know what it feels like to have those smile moments around V8 engines.

As a gamer, I get the same feeling when I complete a particularly challenging mission or part of a game. Grand Theft Auto is full of those smile moments, the humour, the situations, the characters, the mission completion.

Sitting up in my chair, intensely focused, PS4 pad in hand, furiously pushing button combos and then when you just get that move right …? Nailed it!

Followed by "phew," sitting back in my chair, taking a breath and realising I have a grin from ear to ear!
I have no doubt that you are taking yourself back to one of these smile moments as you read and you are actually smiling right now.

The same sense of achievement, the same smile moments happen when you get that project you've loved, at times hated, put blood, sweat, and tears into gets over the finish line. Made all the better because it was on time, and budget, with a team you cared about. You all delivered it.

Learning Takeaway 22;

Enjoying a particular win at anything in life is a requirement for humans to keep moving forward, to learn and grow. Overcoming challenges, together and in real teams, making a difference in our lives is not only fun it's motivational. When this is supported by a systemized and supportive culture within a studio, the team can deliver. When success isn't quite achieved for any particular project, then a desire to improve to overcome and succeed next time is what make a studio truly capable and sets it apart.

Understanding why, what and how the software is developed, gives measurement and confidence to say yes when whatever project is in front of the team and studio is a clear fit and will be a success. Crunch simply put, adds no value to any of the motivations, feelings and capability mentioned here. It may occasionally end in a financial win, but rarely in a personal win for team members.

Questions – Make Notes:

1. *Discuss, at length, with the team a project that was a complete success, deadlines met, creativity, learning, financial gain and was fun to build.*
2. *Document the successful project and break it down into sections, identifying, why, what, where, when, who and how it was a success. Now start to plan how this understanding is the basis of your next project.*

What's next? A move away from the all too familiar? getting to a better place?

Being away from a place where ...

Excessive crunch made you begin and then finally hate the project before it gets finished. The poor planning and continuous change made you start worrying about work all through any days off that you have. Those worried looks from your family, hoping that it will be over soon.

There are no smile moments when a crunched, and poorly planned project finally leaves the studio, just relief and a little knot of fear about the next project coming in.

Greatness and creativity can only be forced for so long, if at all. It is a false economy in every area because sustainability is rarely guaranteed, but crunch will be.

It's time to bring real change to software development, there is a movement towards being more ethical, and for any studio, project management and delivery in a cost-effective way will bring success.

Real teams delivering amazing projects that are fun, creative and enjoyed by all that touch them. Embracing the 3-Stage System to supercharge everything within the studio.

Bringing a "Zero Crunch" culture to an industry that so desperately needs it!

What you need to do next!

If you haven't already, head over to the MLC-Dev support website and take the quick quiz that mirrors all the learning points mentioned in Part 1of this book via 10 simple questions.

This is the best way to explore how many of the great systems already exist in your studio.

If you selected mostly Always as your answer:

You are well on your way to a Zero Crunch position! There will be a few system improvements to make to really supercharge the studios capability.

If you selected mostly Sometimes as your answer:

That's a good score! Work will be needed, but the 3-Stage System will help you develop all the system improvements you need to move towards Zero Crunch.

If you selected mostly Never as your answer:

No matter! It's time to deploy the 3-Stage System for it's most dramatic and greatest effect! This situation is exactly the reason I developed it. For a new way and the benefit of the team and studio to get to Zero Crunch.

Take the quiz, what have you got to lose? Nothing at all, in fact, it is the start of a journey of realisation, improvement and success and it's all within your grasp.

The quiz is over on the website, click the 'Take the Health Check' Button …

www.mlc-devsupport.com

About The Author

Mark Lloyd lives in Scotland on the edge of the Cairngorms with his partner of 25 years, Dianne. After 20 years working in and around the video games industry he now enjoys helping Development Studios be better at what they do.

Credited on over 200 titles including the Grand Theft Auto series and Call of Duty, he spent 12 years as a Rockstar Games Studio Head, building and running Rockstar Lincoln from the ground up. Followed by The Blast Furnace, a 50 veteran studio built for Activision to develop mobile games.

Before the games industry, 12 years aeronautical engineering in the Royal Air Force gave Mark active learning about pressure, discipline, systems and what being part of a real team was — knowing that getting the work right was essential for saving lives as well as saving time and money.

For the last five years, his consultancy business has meant he has shared all that learning and experience with his clients, working within their teams and with managers to help them grow or sustain what they have. All while assisting them in preventing a fall into a never-ending cycle of damaging crunch or project feast and famine.

In his spare time, he volunteered as a mentor for small businesses in Dundee and has been both a Part-Time Lecturer in Project Management and an Enterprise Advisor within schools in the Leeds area.

Here's What People Say About Mark Lloyd

"We were doing well before Mark came into the business. However, as he has worked with the team and I, we have increased our knowledge and capability in every area of the studio. Systems, recruitment and meeting our aim of not crunching! The culture in the studio is better than ever and we are signing new projects with more confidence."

- Stuart Martin – CEO - Hyper Luminal Games

"Mark has spent a number of years helping us to grow operationally with his systems. Building easy to use and high quality processes for the studio. Many of which gave us the tools and to deal with any Publisher. If you are a studio that requires strategic consultation to enhance and achieve your goals, I highly recommend him."

- Simon Iwaniszak – MD - Red Kite Games

"I was part of a small team working with Mark, I appreciated his honesty, his pragmatism, his drive and his integrity. Every team needs someone who is willing to listen to problems, offer support and provide well-considered guidance when appropriate, and that's what Mark brings to the table."

- John Dennis – Design Director – Insight Studios

www.ingramcontent.com/pod-product-compliance
Lightning Source LLC
Chambersburg PA
CBHW070948050326
40689CB00014B/3392